To Maria,

For all your support and understanding.

Previous Praise

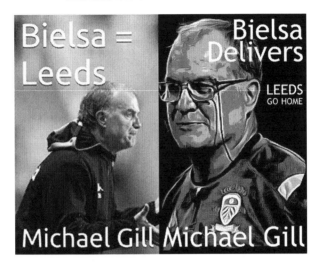

Contents
Bielsa Builds: Leeds March On

Chapter One
Transition Time

When a team triumphs as United did in the extraordinary 2019-20 season, there is normally a period of about a month or so when they can bask in the glory and reflect upon their achievements. Holidays are taken, contracts are sorted out and work begins in preparation for the new season.

No such luxury was afforded to the Whites this time, as the final Championship game against Charlton Athletic took place just over a mere seven weeks before the opening Premier League clash against reigning champions, Liverpool. During this bizarre transitional period, the transfer window and Marcelo Bielsa were the main talking points.

United tried every trick in the book to try and sign Ben White from his parent club, Brighton and Hove Albion on a permanent basis.

All the usual posturing took place with an inflated valuation and reported interest from other clubs, but it eventually became clear that the Seagulls were not going to sell him at any price.

A club official even intimated that Leeds United were seen as a direct rival in a forthcoming relegation struggle.

This was a strange thing to say under any circumstances and reminds me of the man who suffered from a combination of low self-esteem and paranoia; He imagined that he was being followed by the wrong kind of people!

White would have been a great signing not only because of his obvious talent but also for the continuity that his addition would have brought to the team. However, he eventually signed a four-year-deal with his parent club and United fans were left to wish him every success.

The Whites swiftly transferred their attention to the German international, Robin Koch, a central defender from SC Freiburg. The deal passed through without any hitches and was another example of the great work done behind the scenes by Director of Football, Victor Orta.

Orta also secured the services of the Spanish international, Rodrigo Moreno Machado from Valencia. Known simply as 'Rodrigo', he can play either as a traditional striker or out wide. But as we know, he may learn some new tricks from Bielsa!

It was clear that United were going for more valuable players in the transfer market and supporters were assured that there were more signings to come.

As the weeks went by, the question of Bielsa's contract was still unresolved despite several assurances from Andrea Radrizzani, Angus Kinnear and the man himself. Of course, this led to the usual uninformed speculation by certain members of the British press. The lazy hacks drew upon their badly researched cliches:

"He never stays at a club more than two seasons."
"He will leave if he doesn't get what he wants."

He was also linked with a move to Real Madrid, Manchester United and any other club that they could think of. The truth of the matter was more complex, however.

Bielsa was concerned about the increase in media commitments that were required of him as a Premier League coach, but he was also using every hour he had to concentrate on getting his squad ready to compete in the top flight. Thankfully, twenty-four hours before the season's opener against Liverpool, he duly signed a one year extension to his contract.

Owing to the brief nature of the close season, United only played two matches in preparation for life back in the Premier League. The first was an eighty minute affair at Stoke City. This was initially supposed to have been played at the training ground but in the end, both sides graced the hallowed turf of the Bet365 Stadium.

There were no live streams of the game and eager supporters had to keep up with the action on social media. As it turned out, the Whites fielded a depleted side and were beaten 3-0.

Thorpe Arch was the venue for the next game and this one was streamed on LUTV with the familiar voice of Ben Parker.

Leeds United 3-1 Pacos Ferreira
5th September, 2020

Leeds United
Casilla, Douglas, Ayling, Casey, Davis, Struijk, Shackleton, Harrison (Poveda 70), Hernandez (Gotts 73), Roberts, Bamford (Cresswell 88).

This was a strong line up for United, except for the central spine of defence. This was caused principally by the absence of Illan Meslier, Liam Cooper and Robin Koch who were all on international duty.

Stuart Dallas and Gjanni Alioski were unavailable for the same reason, but Tyler Roberts was eligible, having withdrawn from the Wales squad.
Despite this, the team looked as well drilled as ever and the style in which they played was instantly recognisable.

The Whites dominated the first half with good efforts from Bamford, Casey, Harrison and Roberts.

Jordi, The visitors' goalkeeper was on fine form and repelled everything that was thrown at him. Completely against the run of play, the Portuguese side took the lead when SILVA (37) swept a low cross from Joao Amaral into the net.

Their lead was short-lived however, when STRUIJK (39) towered above everyone to head home a perfectly executed Barry Douglas free kick. The Whites wrapped the game up in the second half, when HERNANDEZ (54) fired in a trademark shot from the edge of the box and gave United a deserved lead.

Patrick Bamford then found COSTA (77) with a fine pass, which the lively winger converted. Of the younger players on show, Struijk, Casey and Stevens all caught the eye and substitute Robbie Gotts came close near the end with a great shot. This was a satisfactory warm up game before the real tests began.

My first visit to Anfield was in August 1961, with United and Liverpool both languishing in the old Second Division. The Whites had been relegated in 1960 and the Merseysiders had suffered the indignities of the second tier for much longer, having dropped out of the top flight in 1954.

During the 1950s, Liverpool were undoubtedly the poor relations of the city as they looked enviously across Stanley Park at their rivals, Everton.

But in 1959, they appointed the Huddersfield Town manager Bill Shankly as their new boss. Shankly released no fewer than twenty-four players during his first year at the club. Not only did he fashion a wonderful side, but he built a dynasty that lasted for almost half a century.

Rafael Benitez's appointment in 2004 made him the first Liverpool Manager who had not graduated from the famous 'Boot Room' or formerly played for the club.

Of course, the circumstances of Revie's departure from Elland Road were different as he left quite abruptly to take the England job.

Shankly, on the other hand, retired and succession plans were well in hand at the time that he left. Nevertheless, I have often thought that had the fools who appointed Brian Clough looked to Johnny Giles instead, then things could have been different. Jimmy Armfield did a great job in 'steadying the ship' but by then the damage had already been done.

The Whites had started the 1961-62 season well, with a home win against Charlton Athletic and an away victory at Brighton and Hove Albion.

Nineteen-year-old Billy Bremner scored in both games and the Scotsman had become a regular in the side since his debut at the age of seventeen, when United were in the old First Division.

Player-manager Don Revie was starting his first full season in charge and so there was every reason to be optimistic about their trip to Merseyside.

Along with my late brother, Pat, I boarded our train excited at the prospect of visiting Anfield for the first time. Although my mother's family, the Fenertys, were based in Liverpool, they were keen Evertonians.

I had been to Goodison Park with my cousin, Joe, on visits to their home in Bootle but the other side of Stanley Park was strictly out of bounds.

Our companions on the train were the faithful few who attended away matches. In those dark days, no more than a couple of dozen fans regularly travelled to away games. Eventually we came to know almost all of them.

At that time, the only way that a youngster could get into Anfield at a reduced price was to go into the 'Boy's Pen' which was an infamous compound situated high in a corner of the Kop, unsegregated. I have to say that the banter that my brother and I had to suffer was largely good natured, as we proudly wore our United scarves.

Although these scarves came from the shop, our Mam had carefully embroidered all of the players' names on them. Thankfully, there were not too many transfers in those days!

As Liverpool started to pile on the goals, the mickey-taking took a more cruel turn. Nevertheless, I dread to think what would've happened to us had the Whites won the game or even if they'd scored.

In the end, a 5-0 win for the Reds was deserved as they went on to win the Second Division that season. United narrowly avoided relegation but Don Revie's magic was just starting to work.

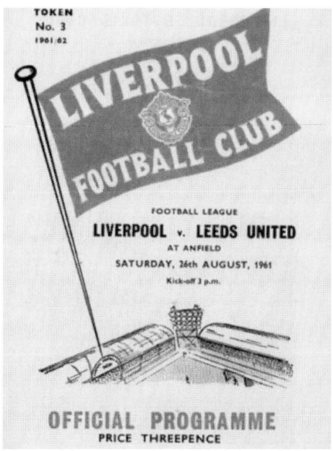

My copy of the programme from Anfield, in August 1961.

Liverpool 4-3 Leeds United
12th September, 2020

Liverpool
Alisson, Alexander-Arnold (Matip 89), Gomez, van Dijk, Robertson, Keita (Fabinho 58), Henderson (Jones 66), Wijnaldum, Salah, Firmino, Mane.

Leeds United
Meslier, Ayling, Koch, Struijk, Dallas, Phillips, Costa, Hernandez (Roberts 62), Klich (Shackleton 81), Harrison, Bamford (Rodrigo 62).

Referee: Michael Oliver

Prior to this game, not one United fan really knew what to expect. This randomly generated fixture could not have been more difficult for United and yet, with zero expectations, they had everything to play for.

The Whites started with an unfamiliar pairing in the centre of defence, due to Ben White's departure and the absence of Liam Cooper who had picked up a calf strain on international duty earlier in the week. Subsequently, Pascal Struijk and Robin Koch took up the vacant positions.

When SALAH (4) flawlessly put away a spot kick after Koch was adjudged to have handled the ball in the penalty area, United looked as if they would really be up against it. But eight minutes later they were level, this time from open play.

Kalvin Phillips found HARRISON (12) with a peach of a pass. The Manchester City loanee raced down the left and passed Alexander-Arnold with some dazzling footwork before smashing the ball into the net with his right foot.

It was the sort of breakaway move that we have seen often in the Championship, but it was even more pleasing to see such a move being executed against Liverpool on their hallowed turf.

The game continued at a breathless pace and once again swung in favour of the Reds. VAN DIJK (20) scored with a trademark bullet header, rising highest to convert a corner. The £75million defender then became the villain ten minutes later, as BAMFORD (30) capitalised on the Dutchman's sloppy error and slipped the ball between him and Alisson.

The Champions only allowed United three minutes breathing space afterwards, as Struijk failed to clear with a header and the clinical SALAH (33) smashed the ball into the top corner.

After half time, the tempo remained at a high level and just as Liverpool seemed to be asserting themselves, the Whites struck back for a third time. KLICH (66) found Helder Costa before racing away to receive the return pass and thumped it into the Liverpool net. The clock ticked away and it seemed that United would be picking up a well-deserved point but sadly, it was not to be.

Since coming on, Rodrigo had been all over the pitch helping his new team mates to stay alive but unfortunately, he was guilty of bringing down Fabinho in the penalty box.

Unsurprisingly SALAH (88) dispatched the ball convincingly past Meslier to complete his hat-trick and break United's hearts. It's rare for any football fan to enjoy a game when their team has been defeated but this was such an occasion.

The media was full of praise for Bielsa's side, although predictably some of it sounded a bit patronising. The clearest message though, was that Leeds United are back and are not prepared to be pushed about by anyone, not even the Champions.

League Position: 9th

"We could have avoided defeat, but Liverpool were the winners. We played according to our style but we struggled to impose ourselves in a lot of periods of the game. On the whole, Liverpool were superior.

Our players were calm, they played a serene game and went into the game confident. To be able to score three goals is a positive thing. We should have created more danger when we attacked.
We also cannot ignore that we conceded four goals. A lot of these goals could have been avoided. I can never be happy in defeat."

-Marcelo Bielsa

If the pre-season game against Pacos Ferreira was an example of how a depleted United team could carry out a well-drilled exercise in a seamless fashion, the next match was the complete opposite. Because of the circumstances, only five senior players (plus Rodrigo and Casilla) were selected to face Hull City in the Carabao Cup Second Round.

Last season was a 'tale of two halves' for the East Yorkshire side, who sat in eighth place at the start of 2020 until an almighty collapse. They only picked up six points from their final twenty games, which meant they finished bottom of the Championship.

Leeds United (8) 1-1 (9) Hull City
16th September, 2020

Leeds United
Casilla, Shackleton, Cresswell, Davis, Douglas, Bogusz (Gotts 78), Poveda, Casey (Struijk 45), Roberts, Alioski, Rodrigo.

Hull City
Ingram, Coyle, Jones, McLoughlin, Elder, Docherty, Batty, Scott, Honeyman (Jones 81), Lewis-Potter (Mayer 45), Wilks (Chadwick 72).

Referee: David Webb

Former United academy product, WILKS (4), put the Whites to the sword early on after capitalising on a breakdown in communication between Kiko Casilla and Barry Douglas.

The former Barnsley man continued to bully and torment the United back line for the remaining time he spent on the pitch.

Kiko Casilla redeemed himself with some good saves afterwards, but Barry Douglas gave the distinct impression that he would rather have been somewhere else.

Oliver Casey was continually having to bolster up the central defence pairing of Leif Davis and Charlie Cresswell, as they struggled to contain the energetic Wilks. As a result, link-up play was lacking in the middle of the field, with rushed clearances frequently going nowhere.

Pascal Struijk's presence added some cohesion to the side, but they still looked like a very pale imitation of the teams that we usually see gracing the white shirt. Ian Poveda also put on a lively performance on the right, but it all seemed too little and too late.

Just when all seemed lost, Barry Douglas found Charlie Cresswell on the right. The youngster headed the ball across the goal in the direction of Rodrigo.

Although the ball just missed the Spanish international, it fell to ALIOSKI (90+3). The North Macedonian, who was having a torrid game up until that point gratefully smashed it into the top corner.

A marathon penalty shoot-out followed and even Kiko Casilla weighed in with a confidently taken penalty. But when Jamie Shackleton fluffed his lines, the away side were handed the opportunity to meet West Ham United in the following round.

"The players didn't gel together very well. This is the responsibility of the coach and as a result, I feel responsible. It wasn't a good game from our team."

-Marcelo Bielsa

Fulham were the next visitors to Elland Road, who also lost their first Premier League fixture. They were beaten 3-0 at home by Arsenal. Although United had triumphed by the same scoreline in the last meeting with Fulham, this was quite flattering to the Whites and a tough challenge was expected.

Leeds United 4-3 Fulham
19th September, 2020

Leeds United
Meslier, Ayling, Koch, Cooper, Dallas, Phillips, Costa, Rodrigo (Roberts 45), Klich, Harrison, Bamford (Alioski 70).

Fulham
Areola, Tete, Hector, Odoi, Bryan, Anguissa, Reed (Lemina 70), Kamara (Kebano 58), Onomah (Decordova-Reid 70), Cavaleiro, Mitrovic.

Referee: Anthony Taylor

Both sides tried to play attractive football from the start and by full time, the possession statistics were shared at 50% each. However, it was United who took the initiative when Phillips sent a bullet-like corner into the box. The Londoners failed to clear their lines and the ball fell to the irrepressible COSTA (5), who gleefully volleyed it into the top corner via the crossbar.

Robin Koch had been looking very polished in defence and is certainly an offensive threat at corners. Unfortunately though, he misjudged his tackle on Joe Bryan and in today's hysterical climate where any form of personal contact is frowned upon, Anthony Taylor pointed to the penalty spot.

MITROVIC (34) made no mistake, although Meslier did dive the right way. Shortly afterwards, United were awarded a penalty of their own. This time Bryan returned the compliment, stroking Bamford's back gently as they rose for the ball. KLICH (41) calmly stroked the resultant spot kick into the Fulham net.

United started the second half like a house on fire. Klich sent BAMFORD (50) away with a cultured through ball and the big striker scored a tidy goal with his weaker right foot.

The Whites soon added to their total with a classic 'Bielsaball' goal which was a joy to watch.

Illan Meslier chipped the ball to Jack Harrison, who headed it to Patrick Bamford. The striker surprised everyone with a sudden burst of speed. Most surprised of all was Denis Odoi, who was left anchored to the turf as Bamford raced down the left. He then crossed it to COSTA (57), who gathered the ball and perfectly dispatched it into the top corner.

That should have been that, but Fulham suddenly found a way back. Substitute DECORDOVA-REID (58) nipped smartly between Cooper and Dallas before smashing it home.

Less than ten minutes later, the clinical MITROVIC (67) rose above United's defence to give the away side fresh hope. Following this, Neeskens Kebano's grazed the outside of the post, although Meslier appeared to have it covered.

Thankfully, the Whites got a grip on themselves and managed to see out another thrilling encounter.

League Position: 10th

"It was a game where we couldn't really show ourselves. In the first half, we defended better but we didn't really create much danger. In the second half we attacked a bit better but we didn't finish the attacks very well. The ten minute spell after the score became 4-3 was our best moment and finally we were able to impose our game a little bit."

-Marcelo Bielsa

A short trip to Sheffield United was the next league fixture. As the Whites had been knocked out of the Carabao Cup, the season continued at quite a leisurely pace with just one game per week.
My first visit to Bramall Lane was on November 5th, 1960. Being close to home, a trip to Sheffield was seen as one of the away matches that I was allowed to attend, provided that I could afford it.

Both my late brother and myself considered ourselves to be fairly well-off in those days, as in addition to our paper rounds we had a nice little job early on Saturday mornings when we would light fires for religious Jewish people as well as turning all the lights on in their houses for them.
There was also another little scam, which I'm deeply ashamed nowadays.

We used to pick up discarded cigarette ends from the street and cut the burnt ends off. We would then shred the tobacco and make roll-ups which we sold to other children at school. I still have a recurring nightmare about elderly men in Leeds with respiratory problems they picked up from smoking these cigarettes when they were children.

Jack Taylor was Leeds United's boss at the start of the decade, having joined from Queens Park Rangers. The Barnsley-born manager presided over United's relegation from the First Division in the previous season and his side were not finding Second Division life any easier.

Apart from the emergence of young Billy Bremner, stalwart Jack Charlton and free-scoring striker John McCole, the Whites didn't have a lot to offer.
They were a collection of average players, as well as old stagers like Ted Burgin, Freddie Goodwin and Don Revie who were coming to the end of their playing careers.

The 'football' part of Bramall Lane only consisted of three sides in those days, as the fourth side faced the County Cricket pitch and was patrolled by an army of ball boys on match days.

The Whites narrowly lost the game 3-2, with Bobby Cameron scoring from the penalty spot. The other goal was scored by Gerry Francis, who was the first black player to represent Leeds United.

Like Albert Johanneson, Francis hailed from South Africa. He was a steady wide player who scored a total of six goals for United in 46 appearances. After his retirement, he emigrated with his family to Toronto where at the time of writing still enjoys good health.

During our journey back to Leeds on the Wallace Arnold coach, we enjoyed seeing all the fireworks light up the night sky as we passed through Barnsley and Wakefield. Guy Fawkes Night, like the Leeds game, turned out to be a bit of a 'damp squib' because when we arrived home, all the local bonfires were fizzling out.

In addition, all the parkin and treacle toffee had been consumed by our hungry friends!

Back in the Championship, our matches against the Blades were always tight encounters. Their talented, but pugnacious manager Chris Wilder certainly saw to that. There was also the added edge in that when it really counted, Wilder's men pipped United to the second automatic promotion spot in 2018-19, condemning the Whites to the play offs and ultimately to failure.

The Blades finished in a respectable ninth place during the 2019-20 Premier League season, however their start to this campaign was less than impressive with defeats to Wolves (2-0) and Aston Villa (1-0). Their big problem was their inability to score goals, but their defence was as sound as ever.

Sheffield United 0-1 Leeds United
27th September, 2020

Sheffield United
Ramsdale, Basham, Ampadu, Robinson, Baldock, Lundstram (Norwood 64), Berge, Osborn, Stevens, McGoldrick (McBurnie 74), Burke (Sharp 74).

Leeds United
Meslier, Cooper, Ayling, Koch, Phillips, Costa (Poveda 66), Klich, Dallas, Harrison, Bamford, Roberts (Rodrigo 45) (Alioski 90).

Referee: Paul Tierney

As expected, this was a tight affair and seemed like being back in the Championship. The Blades were set up to rely on breakaways and if they weren't exactly parking the bus, they were reversing it slowly into the depot.

Nevertheless, both sides had their chances and both goalkeepers certainly earned their wages. It now seems like a long time ago since we put up with the eccentricities of Kiko Casilla and tried to convince ourselves that his lapses could be tolerated, because he was a good shot stopper and that his distribution was superb.

Illan Meslier is David Harvey to Kiko Casilla's Gary Sprake. He is solid, reliable and superior to the Spaniard in every department.

In the first half, Lundstram put the young Frenchman to the test with a rasping shot that looked to be heading for the bottom corner. How Meslier managed to stop the shot at point blank range was bordering on miraculous.

At the other end, Bamford came close and Aaron Ramsdale made a fine save from Stuart Dallas. It really was end to end stuff, although the Whites did have a majority of the possession.

In the second half, Rodrigo replaced the ineffective Tyler Roberts. The experienced forward threw himself into the game and popped up all over the pitch with an energetic performance.

Bielsa's side were starting to dominate and Dallas was unlucky not to score when he rounded Ramsdale, but could not get enough power on his shot, which was cleared by Chris Basham. Ian Poveda's inclusion brought more energy, as they battered away at the Blades defence but it was the Sheffield club who came close shortly afterwards.

Finally there was a breakthrough. Rodrigo, who had his back to the ball sent the ball to Jack Harrison on the left. The Manchester City loanee sent the ball in and found BAMFORD (88) who arrived in time to head the ball in. It later transpired that he struck the ball with his nose, but nobody cared about that.

The Whites then managed the game sensibly and there were no dramas in the remaining minutes.

League Position: 7th

"It was a just result, the first half was pretty even. We could have scored or conceded, but the second half was better for us. We managed to attack better and had close to six or seven opportunities. In that sense, the offensive situation was better."

-Marcelo Bielsa

The final game before the international break was against Manchester City. They had inexplicably lost 5-2 at home to Leicester in the previous match, but nobody was in any doubt that this would prove a stern test for United.

Much had been written about the mutual respect
that Pep Guardiola and Marcelo Bielsa had for each
other and everyone was looking forward to a
mouth-watering encounter.

Leeds United 1-1 Manchester City
3rd October, 2020

Leeds United
Meslier, Ayling, Koch, Cooper, Dallas, Phillips,
Costa, Roberts (Rodrigo 56), Klich (Davis 77),
Alioski (Poveda 45), Bamford.

Manchester City
Ederson, Walker, Dias, Laporte, Mendy (Ake 71),
De Bruyne, Rodrigo, Foden, Torres (Silva 65),
Mahrez (Fernandinho 77), Sterling.

Referee: Mike Dean

This was the game when United proved to the world
that they were a force to be reckoned with. But at
the start of the game, it seemed that they were going
to be overwhelmed. Within minutes, the
prodigiously talented Kevin de Bruyne had hit the
United post with a fiercely struck free kick. Meslier
was completely wrong footed and would not have
reached the shot had it been on target.

The away side continued the onslaught and for
once, it was United who were on the back foot.
Despite a far post header from Gjanni Alioski,
which flew over the bar, something had to give.

When STERLING (17) weaved his way through United's defence and scored a brilliant goal, it seemed that the long-awaited reality check had finally arrived for the Whites.

Somehow, Bielsa's men clawed their way up the slippery pole with Phillips making the most of what little space there was in midfield. Bamford came close and Ayling had a golden opportunity saved by Ederson just before the interval.

In the second half, Poveda and then Rodrigo were introduced replacing Alioski and Roberts. Both of the newcomers had a significant impact on the game. Ian Poveda skipped down the right wing giving the impression that playing against the league's most expensive team was merely routine.

Guardiola silently paid him the greatest compliment by removing Mendy, who was having difficulty in dealing with the lively youngster. Rodrigo also proved to be a much better option in the number 10 spot than the disappointing Tyler Roberts.

The Spain forward put himself about and showed some very deft touches. He showed his sharpness when Ederson could only deflect his clever shot on to and over the bar. Kalvin Phillips then sent in an inviting corner, which caused panic and confusion in the Manchester City defence. Ederson made an uncharacteristic fumble and in the resultant melee, RODRIGO (59) gleefully poked the ball home to put the Whites on level terms.

Cooper was marginally offside when he headed against the post and Rodrigo came close with a header that Ederson tipped against the woodwork. The away side had three penalty appeals rightly turned down as they became increasingly desperate to take all three points.

As the clock ran down, the game swung from end to end but when the final whistle blew, the honours were even.

League Position: 8th

"It would not have been fair if we'd have won this game. It was possible to win the game, but it would not have been fair if we had won. In the beginning, we weren't able to take the ball off them and they were taking the ball off us very easily.

After, we were more aggressive in the duels and as a whole. Apart from defending better we could attack and we attacked well. At the end of the game, we defended as well as attacked but the constant back and forth was more natural for them. At the beginning of the game, it was clear domination from City in all aspects.

In the last fifteen minutes, when they started to dominate again, we managed to produce a different response to the beginning of the first half."

-Marcelo Bielsa

Chapter Two
Bittersweet Battles

United went into the first international break with no small amount of satisfaction. In everyone's eyes, they had exceeded all expectations during their first few games in the top flight.

Nevertheless, it was early days and most experienced fans were not getting carried away. The setbacks and disappointments of recent years have probably scarred many of us, making it difficult to properly enjoy success when it does come.

The most significant event of this short break was the transfer window conclusion. When the window was bolted shut on October 16th, it was perceived that it had been a fruitful set of business for United.

'Marcelo Bielsa Way' was unveiled in July 2020 and connects Trinity Leeds with Commercial Street in the city centre.

Players In

Rodrigo	Valencia	£ 27.00m
Diego Llorente	Real Sociedad	£ 18.00m
Raphinha	Stade Rennais	£ 16.72m
Helder Costa	Wolves	£ 15.93m
Robin Koch	SC Frieburg	£ 11.70m
Illan Meslier	FC Lorient	£ 5.85m
Joe Gelhardt	Wigan Athletic	£ 900,000
Charlie Allen	Linfield	Undisc.
Cody Drameh	Fulham	Undisc.
Jack Harrison	Manchester City	Loan

Players Out (All Loan)

Alfie McCalmont	Oldham Athletic
Barry Douglas	Blackburn Rovers
Bryce Hosannah	Bradford City
Jordan Stevens	Swindon Town
Kun Temenuzhkov	Real Union
Laurens De Bock	Zulte Waregem
Mateusz Bogusz	UD Logrones
Rafa Mujica	Real Oviedo
Robbie Gotts	Lincoln City
Ryan Edmonson	Aberdeen

The first game back was against a Wolves side which was seen as an excellent role model for a promoted team. The Midlands side recorded back-to-back seventh place finishes and secured Europa League qualification during their first season back in the Premier League.

Leeds United 0-1 Wolverhampton Wanderers
19th October, 2020

Leeds United
Meslier, Ayling, Koch, Struijk (Hernandez 75),
Dallas, Phillips, Costa (Poveda 71), Klich, Rodrigo,
Harrison (Raphinha 82), Bamford.

Wolverhampton Wanderers
Patricio, Boly, Coady, Kilman, Semedo, Saiss,
Dendoncker, Moutinho (Neves 82), Neto (Marcal
89), Jimenez, Podence (Traore 65).

Referee: David Coote

Liam Cooper had to pull out of the squad at the last
minute, having picked up a groin injury on
international duty with Scotland. The injury
manifested itself during the warm up and the
dependable Pascal Struijk came in to deputise.

United started with their trademark barnstorming
style but found dangerous shots on goal very hard to
come by, against a well organised team.

Bamford headed the ball into the net but was
adjudged to be offside as he met Jack Harrison's
cross.

Costa, Ayling and Rodrigo all came close but not
close enough against Wolves' well-drilled defence.
Podence then threatened for the away side, but
Meslier was up to anything that was thrown at him.

The second half started with the sides looking more evenly matched. This time Podence crossed to Saiss who smashed the ball past Meslier and into the United net. VAR found Podence to be offside as he crossed the ball, but it was a signal to the Whites that things were getting too close for comfort.

Shortly afterwards, disaster struck. The United defence struggled with the pace and trickery of JIMENEZ (70), who weaved through and found the bottom left hand corner with the help of a massive deflection off Kalvin Phillips.

In the last twenty minutes, Ian Poveda and Pablo Hernandez joined the fray, followed later by new signing Raphinha which seemed to liven United up.

Eight minutes from the end, the Brazilian sent a fine cut back to Ian Poveda whose shot was blocked and spun to Rodrigo, who couldn't quite swing around to get a good connection.

League Position: 10th

"Given how the game went, we thought we did enough to create a lead. When an offensive team doesn't take their chances, the opponent reads this and they start to grow in confidence. The game was very physical, there were many interruptions and it was difficult to find continuity in the game. In the second half we lost some offensive capability."

-Marcelo Bielsa

Next up were Aston Villa who had put seven goals past Liverpool a fortnight before, in a season of increasingly bizarre Premier League results. The Villains narrowly avoided relegation in the previous season, but had won all four of their opening league games before facing United.

After the game against Wolves, some of the more fainthearted fans were worried whether United could overcome the Midlanders. It also didn't help that there were four days between the matches, as a result of some odd scheduling which even BT Sport and Sky would have difficulty explaining!

The fixture was also a casualty of the Premier League's greedy collaboration with broadcasters and would cost fans £14.95 for the privilege of watching it live on television. This resulted in a significant number of supporters refusing to pay the fee, donating the money to food banks instead.

This was a successful gesture which led to the Premier League and broadcasters agreeing to screen the games for free using some of the terrestrial channels and Amazon to share the load.

This came into force prior to the next international break and was widely welcomed by fans. Although you couldn't help but think that had the clubs and broadcasters been a little less greedy, then they could have continued to collect some form of payment for the pay-per-view matches.

Aston Villa 0-3 Leeds United
23rd October, 2020

Aston Villa
Martinez, Cash, Konsa, Mings, Target, McGinn,
Luiz, Trezeguet (Traore 66), Barkley, Grealish,
Watkins.

Leeds United
Meslier, Dallas, Koch, Ayling, Alioski, Costa
(Raphinha 83), Struijk (Shackleton 21), Klich,
Harrison, Rodrigo (Hernandez 79), Bamford.

Referee: Paul Tierney

Both Liam Cooper and Kalvin Phillips were absent
for this match, which saw Luke Ayling deputise as
captain in the centre of defence. Pascal Struijk
slotted in to play the defensive midfield role.

There was early encouragement for the Whites, as
Harrison sent Alioski away and the North
Macedonian put a cross in for Bamford, who
headed just wide. As usual, Jack Grealish was
proving to be a handful and Struijk was struggling
to contain him.

After only ten minutes, the Dutch youngster picked
up a yellow card for a clumsy tackle and shortly
afterwards, he was pulled up for another foul.
There's not many players better at drawing fouls
than Jack Grealish and although some are genuine,
some are very dubious.

It did seem that if things continued, 'slippery Jack' would have little difficulty in getting Struijk sent off.

Ten minutes later, the young defender was substituted and replaced by Jamie Shackleton, who eased himself into the side. Yet another problem for United in this key position, but the Whites carried on regardless.

Shortly afterwards, Grealish had a penalty shout as Helder Costa passed by the back of him, but VAR confirmed that there had been no contact. Both sides looked lively before the break, with chances coming at both ends of the pitch.

The second half began with two close efforts from Villa, as Grealish brought the best out of Illan Meslier and Konsa also made the Frenchman stretch from the resulting corner.

But United were ramping up the pressure and reaped the rewards when Shackleton sent Rodrigo away. The Spain international played a quick exchange with Harrison before shooting towards goal. Martinez could only parry the ball to BAMFORD (55), who gratefully tucked it home.

Twelve minutes later, BAMFORD (67) received the ball with his back to the goal twenty-five yards out. In one movement, the big striker spun around and curled his shot into the top corner, giving Martinez no chance at all.

There was no stopping BAMFORD (74) as he received an assist from Helder Costa in the crowded Villa penalty area and with another 'soft shoe shuffle' somehow found space to pick his spot in the other top corner of the net.

This was a fine performance from United and you couldn't help but think that the home side might have been a little overconfident, as they went into this game.

League Position: 6th

"We've been together as a group for two-and-a-half years now so the group is homogenous and it's easier for everyone to assimilate their roles.

From my point of view, Bamford is a player with a lot of qualities. He produces a lot more danger than he concretes. If he continues to improve his efficiency, he will receive greater plaudits."

-Marcelo Bielsa

In 2016, unfashionable Leicester City had broken the stranglehold applied by Manchester City, Chelsea and Manchester United by winning the Premier League.

The Foxes were promoted from the Championship as title winners in 2013-14 and many pundits had said that this sort of breakthrough would never happen in the modern game.

Leeds United 1-4 Leicester City
2nd November, 2020

Leeds United
Meslier, Ayling, Koch, Cooper, Dallas (Alioski 81),
Klich, Costa, Hernandez (Roberts 67), Shackleton
(Poveda 45), Harrison, Bamford.

Leicester City
Schmeichel, Justin, Fofana, Fuchs, Albrighton,
Tielemans, Mendy, Thomas, Praet (Maddison 63),
Barnes (Under 71), Vardy (Morgan 85).

Referee: Andre Marriner

The game started terribly for United and carried on
in a similar vein. It was a filthy night with the rain
lashing down and the fact that Elland Road was
empty only added to the bleakness of the occasion.

Rodrigo was unavailable, after coming in contact
with a family member who had tested positive for
COVID-19. United's record signing was replaced
by Pablo Hernandez. As Kalvin Phillips was also
still absent with his shoulder injury, Jamie
Shackleton kept his place after his impressive
performance against Aston Villa.

Before either side had time to catch their breath, the
ball was in the United net. Robin Koch attempted to
pass back to Illan Meslier but the ball skidded
across the surface before coming to a sloshing halt,
leaving the young keeper stranded.

The clinical Jamie Vardy rounded the youngster, before squaring the ball to BARNES (3) who had the simple task of tapping it in to the net. Leicester then sat back and as passes from Klich and Hernandez repeatedly went astray, the Midlanders played the game in the way that they wanted to.

Once again, Vardy was the architect of a Foxes goal, as the veteran striker appeared at the near post and sent a diving header across the goal. Meslier saved brilliantly, but could only parry the ball to TIELEMANS (21) who made no mistake with his follow up.

United's goal chances were few and far between as the away side soaked up the pressure and frustrated Bielsa's men at every turn.

In an effort to pick the lock on Leicester's reinforced door, Ian Poveda replaced Jamie Shackleton and for a brief period it seemed to make the Whites look more dangerous.

DALLAS (50) received the ball from a short corner and attempted to cross the ball back into the danger area. Incredulously he watched as the ball bounced and crept just inside the far post.

Hernandez was next to have a crack and after a bit of trademark wizardry, he smashed the ball on to the post. This happening seemed to knock the wind out of the United side and twelve minutes later, he was replaced by Tyler Roberts.

Hernandez showed his anger at the substitution and it was hard not to have sympathy with the little Spaniard, because if you discounted the freakish goal his effort was the only one that had troubled the Foxes in any way.

Tyler Roberts came on and was unable to make a significant contribution to the game. Having suffered badly from injuries last season, the youngster seems to have lost his way.

Although far less impressive in the second half, Leicester were working their way back into the game and scored again shortly afterwards.

Maddison sent Under through and the Turkish international slipped the ball past Meslier to the oncoming VARDY (76), who took his reward by simply passing the ball into an empty net.

Worse was to come as Klich made a challenge on Maddison inside the penalty area, which was deemed to be a foul. Andre Marriner had missed the incident, but he was called to the VAR monitor and after studying the footage, pointed to the spot.

TIELEMANS (90+1) made no mistake as he claimed his second goal of the evening. Sadly, the result was every bit as comprehensive as the scoreline suggested.

League Position: 12th

"I didn't distribute the players correctly on the field. It was difficult for us to win the ball back and this caused us to defend poorly. We had an hour to attack; the last fifteen minutes of the first half and the whole of the second half. We couldn't manage to cause any harm, any damage to the opponent's defence. We didn't create enough chances given the amount of possession we had over this hour."

-Marcelo Bielsa

If the Leicester City game was an important lesson learned, the following match was something else entirely. Although the results were identical, you were left feeling that United could have come away from this match with a point.

Memorable games involving the Whites at Selhurst Park are few and far between, but the previous meeting stays in my memory for all the wrong reasons. Neil Warnock was unveiled as the new Leeds United manager in February 2012 after Ken Bates had disposed of Simon Grayson because of a poor run of results.

Warnock's appointment was not a popular one and he did little to endear himself to the United faithful. Admittedly, a lot of the decisions like the sale of Robert Snodgrass to Norwich, could hardly have been laid at Warnock's door. It was just that he went about his business with an overconfident bluster which was not borne out by his actions or the performance of the team.

In March 2013, United visited Crystal Palace and prior to the game, I found myself at the Clifton Arms which had a 'Home Fans Only' sign outside.

Although the Crystal Palace fans didn't have a reputation for aggression or violence, I wanted to make sure that I was served and ordering my drink with a Yorkshire accent would be a dead giveaway.

I was a tiny, little thin fellow as a child until I had a growth spurt in my teenage years. Because of this, I had developed an ability to make people laugh by making jokes and doing funny voices.

This was an infinitely a better choice than being beaten up by the many bullies, who if not sponsored by the school were certainly not discouraged.

I never managed to do a faux cockney accent and did not trust myself with this. I ordered a pint in my best Dublin accent, which I thought would suffice for this occasion.

Unfortunately, it was not the best choice.
"Ah, a fellow Dub. What part are yeh from?" The barman enquired.
"Drumcondra. But it was a long time ago." I said.
"Well, yeh never lost it me owld son." He replied.

Luckily, the pub was very busy and I was able to retreat before making sure that when I returned to the bar, I would be served by someone else!

A few weeks earlier, another fans' favourite had been sold to Norwich City. Luciano Becchio was a regular goal scorer and provided some bright moments in a very dark era for United.

The Argentinian went to Carrow Road in exchange for the former Millwall striker, Steve Morison, and an undisclosed payment. Although Morison had scored plenty of goals for the South London side, his record with the Canaries was less impressive.

Despite scoring nine goals in his first season with the East Anglian side, his tally was only one out of nineteen games in the 2012-13 season.

It goes without saying that Warnock tried to convince everybody that he had received the better bargain. Morison later admitted that he had never wanted to come to United and had been sold against his will.

The 2013 game at Selhurst Park was a lively 2-2 draw and Morison surprised everyone by scoring both of the Whites' goals. After his second, he made an ironic gesture to the United fans.

It wasn't quite as offensive as Mark Aizlewood's two fingers to the Kop, but it did nothing to endear him to the Elland Road faithful.

Morison only went on to score two more goals for United, before returning to his beloved Millwall.

Crystal Palace 4-1 Leeds United
7th November, 2020

Crystal Palace
Guaita, Clyne, Kouyate, Dann, van Aanholt, Townsend (Schlupp 71), Riedewald (McCarthy 77), McArthur, Eze, Ayew (Benteke 85), Zaha.

Leeds United
Meslier, Ayling, Koch, Cooper, Dallas, Struijk (Roberts 71), Alioski, Costa (Raphinha 45), Klich, Harrison, Bamford.

Referee: Chris Kavanagh

Pascal Struijk was recalled to take on the crucial role of holding midfielder, as Kalvin Phillips continued to be absent owing to his shoulder injury. The dependable Gjanni Alioski was also given a start as United sought to complete a fixture before the international break. Thankfully, this was the last scheduled disruption until March 2021.

The wily and experienced Roy Hodgson had started his fourth season as Palace manager, despite a relatively poor showing in the previous campaign.

Palace were awarded a corner after a counterattack and Eze picked up the ball, before crossing it for DANN (12) to head home. United's response was rapid as Luke Ayling worked the ball out of defence and Mateusz Klich sent a lovely through ball to Patrick Bamford, who smashed the ball into the net.

42

Sadly the effort was adjudged to be offside. The latest outrage from the VAR system ruled that Bamford's arm was in an offside position, as he pointed to the spot where he wanted the Polish international to put the ball.

This was one of the craziest decisions yet to come from this flawed system and was universally condemned by pundits and former referees alike. Had the goal been allowed, it would have come at a crucial stage of the game, but it wasn't to be.

Very shortly afterwards, Robin Koch and Eberechi Eze came together in a scuffle at the edge of the United area. EZE (22) then picked himself up and found the top corner of Meslier's goal to give the Eagles another goal.

In a move involving the same personnel to the one which produced the disallowed goal, Ayling found Klich, who then headed the ball to BAMFORD (25). The big striker gave himself just enough space to whip the ball past Guaita.

Fate was once again unkind to the Whites just before half time, as van Aanholt sent a speculative cross into the United penalty area. The ball cannoned off the unfortunate COSTA (42), to restore the home side's two goal lead.

Bielsa's men were subdued in the second half and played like a team smarting from injustice and bad luck.

Pascal Struijk came close with a header from a Jack Harrison corner, but that was the closest that the Whites came to reducing the deficit.

Although the introduction of Raphinha livened the side, far too many moves were breaking down before the forwards had the opportunity to do anything about them.

Almost inevitably, AYEW (70) scored one off the back post after rounding Jack Harrison, which put the game to bed once and for all.

It could have been worse as Eze and Zaha terrorised the Whites' defence and most United fans must have greeted the final whistle with a sigh of relief. Phillips was sadly missed and replacing him against the faster sides has proved to be a big problem.

As it turned out, United would not fall below the league position they found themselves in following this defeat to Crystal Palace.

League Position: 15th

"The defeat is fair but the difference is exaggerated and the goals Crystal Palace scored, arrived at the time when we deserved to score. Whatever the referee whistles, he whistles and I never comment on his decision. If the rules need to be changed, there's lots of people dedicated to this."

-Marcelo Bielsa

When the Whites played Arsenal in the FA Cup in January 2020, they certainly competed well. United dominated the first half and did everything but score. As expected though, the home side pulled themselves together in the second half and narrowly won the game, 1-0.

The Whites received almost universal approval for their performance as the plaudits came thick and fast. This time around however, they were not looking for a 'pat on the back' but simply the three points, after their last two reverses.

Leeds United 0-0 Arsenal
22nd November, 2020

Leeds United
Meslier, Ayling (Rodrigo 70), Koch, Cooper, Alioski, Phillips, Raphinha, Klich, Dallas, Harrison (Poveda 80), Bamford.

Arsenal
Leno, Bellerin, Holding, Gabriel, Tierney, Ceballos, Xhaka, Pepe, Willock (Saka 57) (Maitland-Niles 90), Willian (Nelson 45), Aubameyang.

Referee: Anthony Taylor

Conceding goals rather than being unable to score them had been United's problem in the previous two games. This game was the opposite and the Whites were unlucky not to bag all three points.

Although, they must have taken some satisfaction in a much improved defensive performance.

The Whites squandered chance after chance in the first half with wayward efforts from Klich and Dallas. Most of the side were also guilty of wasting passes in a closely fought struggle.

Six minutes into the second half, Nicholas Pepe was sent off after putting his head too close to Gjanni Alioski. This infringement was not as dramatic as the North Macedonian made out, but it was still an unacceptable clash in the modern game.

How a player of Pepe's experience could fall into such a trap is a mystery. We all know that Alioski is a professional agitator but this was ridiculous. From then on, United came much closer with Bamford, Raphinha and Rodrigo taking the 'paint off the woodwork' on no fewer than three occasions.

Near the end of the match, Saka could have stolen the points for Arsenal, as he found himself one-on-one with Illan Meslier. The young Frenchman was having none of this, as he showed superb judgement and timing to push the ball out of harm's reach without risking an infringement.

League Position: 14th

"The game had two moments. The first hour where we played eleven versus eleven, in which we dominated and did not allow the opponent to react.

Also, the final half hour when the dominance was even more clear. Offensively we did enough to establish a lead.

When we played eleven against eleven, there were some difficult battles to control in defence as well as attack. In this sense we were able to establish some positive duels. When the attacks all finished in front of goal in the final half hour we had resources to create chances for some danger."

-Marcelo Bielsa

Football is filled with remarkable coincidences but one of the oddest is the relationship between Everton and Leeds United.

I had been to see the Toffees play a couple of times with my Liverpool-based cousin, Joe Fenerty. But my first visit to support the Whites was in November 1964 when the notorious 'Battle of Goodison' took place.

United were newly promoted from the old Second Division and were already making a name for themselves, not only as a good footballing side but as an uncompromising side physically.

We had the luxury of travelling by car to this game, joining Alf Fisher, David Drake and 'Old George'. After Alf had given a horrible urchin the obligatory few coins to 'look after' the car, we made our way to the ground not knowing what was about to ensue.

47

In an era when you had to be able to take a few knocks as well as hand them out, United were perfectly capable of doing both. One of the main protagonists in this particular encounter was the diminutive midfielder, Bobby Collins.

Three years earlier, Collins had signed for the Whites at the age of thirty-one after Everton manager, Harry Catterick, had deemed him surplus to requirements.

This had hurt the little Scot badly as fitness was never an issue with him. He had gone on to prove his worth with United and was widely regarded as Don Revie's most influential signing.

The game started with a few niggles, but was only four minutes old when Sandy Brown of Everton was sent off for punching Johnny Giles in the face. He claimed that the Irishman had gone way over the top in a tackle and had left him with stud marks on his chest.

On fifteen minutes, Collins took a free kick just outside the penalty area and to the delight of the United fans it was headed home by another Scot, Willie Bell. He was a solid enough full back but wasn't noted for his goalscoring.

A home supporter then ran on to the pitch but was restrained by Johnny Morrissey of Everton, who prevented him from getting to Billy Bremner and Norman Hunter.

The on-pitch battles continued and culminated with Bell clattering Everton's Derek Temple, who was carried off on a stretcher. In his spare time, Willie Bell coached a number of Sunday league teams, including the one that I played for.

On the rare occasions that you managed to get the ball off him, he would scythe you down and explain that he couldn't help it!

Bell, Les Cocker and referee Derek Stokes were then pelted with missiles as pandemonium broke out. Only thirty-nine minutes had elapsed but Stokes had had enough and in an unprecedented decision, he ordered both teams off the pitch.

Tannoy announcements were made that the game would be abandoned if there was any more trouble. Play resumed after ten minutes, but not before Brian Labone and Bobby Collins appealed to both sets of supporters to stay calm.

The violence continued on the pitch but there were no more invasions from supporters, even at the end of the game.

Incredibly, the only other player to be disciplined was Hunter who received a booking.

The Whites refused to be put off their game and Bell's goal was enough to send them back to Yorkshire as worthy winners. Thankfully, we didn't get into any trouble ourselves that day as well.

United were to meet Everton three more times that season, beating them 4-1 in the reverse league fixture and triumphing 2-1 at Goodison in front of a 65,000 crowd in the FA Cup. The first tie was drawn 1-1 at Elland Road.

Nearly twenty six years later in August 1990, Howard Wilkinson's newly promoted Whites travelled to Goodison Park to commence their First Division campaign.

By this time, I was based in Hertfordshire but I wasn't going to miss this match for anybody. I had some business in Keighley on the Saturday morning but this would leave me plenty of time to pop over to Liverpool.

On the Friday night, I visited The Kashmir Restaurant which is an old favourite and still a Bradford institution to this day. Deciding on an early night, I headed for the Midland Hotel on Forster Square where I had checked in previously.

I was looking forward to a nice, cooked breakfast in the morning but noticed a strange smell in the restaurant. It didn't seem too unpleasant an odour, that is until I realised what it was.

Apparently there was some sort of a Bodybuilders convention being held in the city and I was being joined for breakfast by about fifty of them, both male and female.

The dress code seemed to be jogging pants and a flimsy singlet which did nothing to contain their bulging muscles.

They had all oiled their bodies to a high gloss and the oil was the cause of the smell. I didn't stay too long and the bacon, eggs and sausages didn't taste quite as well as I had imagined that they would.

I arrived at Goodison at around two o'clock and had time to catch up with a few old friends before the match. The main talking point of the day was the absence of Vinnie Jones.

The former Wimbledon man had been a talismanic figure in the promotion battle the previous season and his absence was not due to injury.

United had signed Gary McAllister from Leicester City to fulfil the creative midfield role, which saw Jones move on to Sheffield United not long after.

Within twenty minutes, United had gone ahead with goals from Chris Whyte and Gary Speed and went into the break having experienced the luxury of an Everton missed penalty.

Shortly after half time, Everton keeper Neville Southall walked back on to the pitch and sat down resting his back against one of the goalposts at the United end. Clearly, he didn't think that the half time team talk applied to him.

The Whites pushed further ahead in the second half, thanks to Imre Varadi, before conceding two goals themselves. The last thirteen minutes were tense, but Wilkinson's men held out and made a big impression on the First Division, finishing in fourth place that season.

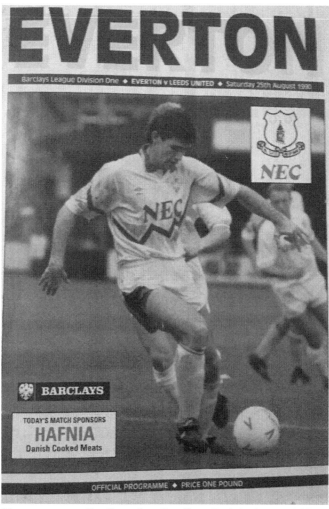

The programme I collected at Goodison Park in August 1990.

Everton 0-1 Leeds United
28th November, 2020

Everton
Pickford, Godfrey, Keane, Holgate (Bernard 82), Davies (Delph 61), Doucoure, Allan, Iwobi (Gomes 66), Rodriguez, Calvert-Lewin, Richarlison.

Leeds United
Meslier, Ayling, Koch, Cooper, Dallas, Raphinha (Poveda 84), Klich, Phillips, Alioski, Harrison (Costa 81), Bamford (Rodrigo 90).

Referee: Chris Kavanagh

Following the clash with Arsenal, this was another really tight game. Both sides possessed the wherewithal to score goals, but also had great defences and in particular, the goalkeepers. Jordan Pickford is England's number one and you feel that it is only a matter of time before Illan Meslier becomes first choice for France.

Everton had made their best start to a Premier League campaign but had faltered recently, losing three games in a row before narrowly beating a fragile looking Fulham side.

Meslier saved a tricky deflection from Richarlison before Pickford saved in quick succession from Bamford and Raphinha. Both Rodriguez and Richarlison had the ball in the net, but both efforts were rightly ruled out for offside.

In the second half, play once again swung both ways with Calvert-Lewin coming close for Everton and Bamford for the Whites. As time was running out, United struck the knockout punch.

RAPHINHA (79) had the ball twenty-five yards out and appeared to be looking to make a telling pass, but instead raised his head and found the bottom corner giving Pickford no chance. In their true tradition, the Whites carried on attacking until the end and Helder Costa was unlucky not to double their lead in the dying minutes.

This was another triumph for Marcelo Bielsa's ethics and overall philosophy.

League Position: 12th

"You saw that Everton has a front line that can all unbalance. James Rodriguez can unbalance, Calvert-Lewin can unbalance, Richarlison as well.

We made a conscious effort to have someone close to Rodriguez throughout so that he was not able to do the thing that he likes to do the most, which is to turn and send those passes in behind. Despite the efforts of Dallas, Cooper and Klich he was a player who was very difficult to neutralise.

Raphinha is a player who has adapted very quickly to the Premier League. Victor Orta, who chose him and brought him here, had identified that he has the necessary qualities to adapt to the Premier League.

He's a player who can unbalance, who's potent and moves all around the pitch."

-Marcelo Bielsa

Chapter Three
Goals Galore

In a season filled with stern tests, the next game was going to be as tough a test as any previously encountered by the Whites. There had been quite a lot of history between the two clubs and this was augmented by the fact that their manager was none other than Frank Lampard.

He had managed Derby County during 'Spygate' and the epic tussles that had taken place in the 2018-19 Championship campaign. Prior to this season, the Blues spent around £200m and were expected to qualify for the Champions League.

Chelsea 3-1 Leeds United
5th December, 2020

Chelsea
Mendy, James, Zouma, Silva, Chilwell, Havertz (Kovacic 67), Kante, Mount, Ziyech (Pulisic 30), Giroud (Abraham 79), Werner.

Leeds United
Meslier, Ayling, Koch (Llorente 9), Cooper, Alioski (Rodrigo 69), Raphinha, Dallas, Phillips, Harrison (Poveda 57), Klich, Bamford.

Referee: Kevin Friend

United approached the game with their usual gusto and BAMFORD (4) received a beautiful through ball from Kalvin Phillips, before rounding Edouard Mendy to slip the ball in for the opening goal. A few minutes later, Robin Koch broke down and had to limp off the field.

It emerged that the central defender had been shielding a knee injury since the Liverpool game and that he would need to have surgery. The German was replaced by Diego Llorente, who had only just returned from injury himself. It's unlikely that he would have been risked if it had not been for the desperate situation.

From a corner, Olivier Giroud made a connection which looked to be heading for the corner. This was until Timo Werner, who was practically standing on the goal line, somehow managed to smash the ball against the bar and eventually to safety.

Bamford then shot the ball over the bar after good work from Klich. This was before Alioski hit the post, although it wouldn't have counted as Ayling was judged to be offside in the build up.

Almost inevitably, Chelsea then equalised as GIROUD (27) steered the ball past Meslier after a fine move involving Havertz, Ziyech and James. The Blues were picking up far too many loose balls in midfield and United were finding it very difficult to play out from the back.

In the second half, the Whites even resorted to the long ball in an attempt to circumvent the midfield battle. When they did revert to their normal game, United gave the ball away too many times as the pressure continued to mount.

Werner produced a fine double save from Meslier and from the resulting corner, ZOUMA (61) converted with a firmly struck header.

Rodrigo and Poveda both worked their socks off after being introduced and the former Manchester City man was extremely unlucky not to have been awarded a penalty, after being tripped by Ben Chilwell.

Instead of throwing himself to the floor, the youngster picked himself up and got a shot in which Mendy saved well. It's a sad feature of the modern game that had Poveda stayed down, the Whites would have probably been awarded a spot kick.

In the dying seconds of the game, Werner sent a low cross in to PULISIC (90+3) who did the rest and finally put the game beyond United's grasp.
The Whites were beaten by the better side and could have few complaints about the result.

League Position: 14th

"I thought the result was fair. What we lacked was the ability to recover the ball in the initial phase of the game, when Chelsea played out from the back.

It was a game that was difficult to defend, given the quality of the opponent's forwards. Chelsea are one of the most important teams in the league."

-Marcelo Bielsa

The next match at Elland Road was against David Moyes' West Ham United. Prior to this game, the Glaswegian had won an impressive four out of five games against the Whites in the Premier League. His current side were in relatively good form as well and were determined to further polish the record of their veteran manager against United.

Leeds United 1-2 West Ham United
11th December, 2020

Leeds United
Meslier, Dallas, Ayling, Cooper, Alioski (Shackleton 45), Phillips, Raphinha, Rodrigo, Klich, Harrison (Costa 45), Bamford (Roberts 74).

West Ham United
Fabianski, Coufal, Balbuena, Ogbonna, Cresswell, Rice, Soucek, Bowen (Johnson 85), Benrahma (Noble 84), Fornals (Snodgrass 90+5), Haller.

Referee: Michael Oliver

The Whites got off to just the kind of start that they were hoping for. Liam Cooper sent a fine through ball to Patrick Bamford, who raced forward with only the Hammers keeper Fabianski to beat.

The Polish international unhesitatingly pulled the striker down, leaving the referee with no choice but to point to the penalty spot.

Mateusz Klich had demonstrated cool confidence with his spot kicks, but this effort could better be described as lukewarm. He rolled the ball accurately but without any strength to Fabianski's right and left the keeper with the easy task of retrieving it.

Thankfully, the VAR system spotted that the Hammers goalkeeper had moved off his line and at the second time of asking, KLICH (6) made no mistake with his shot.

Although Said Benrahma and Jarrod Bowen were giving the home defence a tough time from the flanks, Moyes' men drew level as the result of a corner. SOUCEK (25) rose above Stuart Dallas to head the ball in at the far post.

At half time, Jack Harrison and Gjanni Alioski were replaced by Helder Costa and Jamie Shackleton. Although the latter seemed to add some energy to the side, the game was locked in a dour stalemate.

The London club had the better of the few chances which did come, as Fabian Balbuena was thwarted only by a first class save from Illan Meslier. Helder Costa had failed to make much of an impact on the game and when he finally did, it was a negative one after conceding an unnecessary free kick on the edge of the area.

Cresswell dispatched it to the far post and the experienced OGBONNA (80) rose to head the ball in to the goal.

The Whites went on to lose their second game in a row. Once again, a combination of ineffective finishing and the failure to defend set pieces had been the achilles heel. In contrast, the Hammers were organised and workmanlike.

League Position: 14th

"There are no mysteries to the things that we have to do. The set-pieces can be perfected by continually training them. You have to reproduce what happens in the game during a training session. We will continue insisting on this until we can resolve the problem.

What's happening is not excusing me with that being done. This problem we're having, we've already had it before in the past, we resolved it and now it's happening again."

-Marcelo Bielsa

Five days later, the Whites were at home again. Newcastle United were the visitors and it was felt that this type of fixture was one that Bielsa's men ought to be taking three points from. After losing to Chelsea, the Magpies recorded wins against Crystal Palace and West Bromwich Albion.

Despite a recent bout of COVID-19 in the camp, they were expected to provide tough opposition.

Before this game, many of the pundits were trotting out the usual rubbish about United being exhausted, burnt out and a spent force. The events that followed, proved them right. That is of course, if they were referring to Newcastle United.

Leeds United 5-2 Newcastle United
16th December, 2020

Leeds United
Meslier, Dallas, Ayling, Cooper, Alioski, Phillips, Raphinha, Rodrigo (Hernandez 82), Klich (Shackleton 89), Harrison, Bamford (Roberts 83).

Newcastle United
Darlow, Murphy, Fernandez, Clark, Lewis, Hendrick (Krafth 62), Longstaff, Hayden, Fraser (Almiron 75), Wilson, Joelinton (Gayle 74).

Referee: Simon Hooper

Rodrigo and Raphinha started energetically and both had shots on goal in the early stages. Shortly afterwards though, tragedy struck after Rodrigo failed to find Raphinha with a pass.

Fraser picked the ball up for the Magpies, before finding Wilson. The striker then flicked the ball on to KENDRICK (26), who slotted home to put the Geordies in front.

Raphinha was once again heavily involved in attack for the Whites. After coming close on a couple of occasions, his next action was more decisive. The Brazilian sent a great cross in for Rodrigo, who struck the crossbar. Fortunately, BAMFORD (35) was in the right place as he rose above the ball to head it firmly downwards into the net.

Honours were even at half time and this had the look of a match that could swing either way. There was a coming together between Liam Cooper and Callum Wilson, but a penalty claim was denied following a VAR check.

United's next goal was very easy on the eye after Rodrigo showed great close control and sent the ball down the left for Jack Harrison.

The Manchester City loanee showed great athleticism as he reached the ball just before it passed the line. His cross was met with a diving header from RODRIGO (61) who rounded off the move which he had initiated.

However, the Magpies stayed resilient and a few minutes later were level. This time, CLARK (65) rose above Liam Cooper from a corner to make the scores two all.

Jack Harrison was on fire as he pulled the ball back for Mateusz Klich to cross in, where DALLAS (77) arrived at the far post to head home.

Not long afterwards, a Kalvin Phillips clearance found Raphinha who raced clear. He then found substitute Pablo Hernandez on the overlap and the Spanish wizard played in ALIOSKI (85), to smash it in from twelve yards. HARRISON (88) then capped off a great display by finding the top corner from long range.

League Position: 13th

"In both halves, we created plenty of chances but in the second half we were more efficient. The team carried on playing in a calm and organised manner after they levelled the game and scored goals when we needed to. We managed the ball very patiently. That's what most impressed me about the team."

-Marcelo Bielsa

The next game was one that many fans had been waiting a long time for. In 2010, League One Leeds United were drawn to face their greatest rivals and reigning English champions, Manchester United in the FA Cup Third Round.

Nine thousand away tickets were allocated and nobody gave the Whites a chance at Old Trafford.

But Jermaine Beckford went full stretch to score the only goal of the game. By doing this, the striker placed himself into the Elland Road Hall of Fame. Regrettably, I was unable to attend that match.

But I did manage to stand in the Stretford end and watch Leeds Rhinos defeat Wigan Warriors 22-20 in the 2015 Super League Grand Final.

That season, the Rhinos also won the Challenge Cup and the League Leaders' Trophy. The 'Blessed Trinity' of Kevin Sinfield, Rob Burrow and Danny Maguire were at the height of their powers. Sadly, I'm unlikely to witness the likes of them ever again.

Despite scoring five and being mightily impressive in the last fixture, nobody harboured any illusions about the Whites brushing aside Manchester United. Not even the 2020 version of the team.

Manchester United 6-2 Leeds United
20th December, 2020

Manchester United
De Gea, Wan-Bissaka, Lindelof, Maguire, Shaw (Telles 60), McTominay, Fred, James, Fernandes (van de Beek 71), Rashford (Cavani 71), Martial.

Leeds United
Meslier, Dallas, Ayling, Cooper (Davis 72), Alioski, Phillips (Struijk 45), Raphinha, Rodrigo, Klich (Shackleton 45), Harrison, Bamford.

Referee: Anthony Taylor

No sooner had the game kicked off that the Whites found themselves in big trouble.

MCTOMINAY (2) picked up a fine pass from Bruno Fernandes and sent a shot from outside of the box to the bottom right hand corner of Meslier's goal. Less than a minute later, the talented young Scot was at it again.

Anthony Martial played a clever through ball and MCTOMINAY (3) ran in to smash home a second. Punch drunk and reeling from the shock, the Whites were struggling to impose their normal game.

Worse was to come, when Luke Ayling made a half hearted attempt at dispossessing Martial in the area. The ball fell to FERNANDES (20), who drilled the ball in to the net. LINDELOF (37) then slipped past Kalvin Phillips from a corner to make it four. The Whites did respond quickly though, as COOPER (42) headed home a Raphinha corner.

Half time came as something of a relief and at the least it gave the Whites a chance to get their breath back. Kalvin Phillips and Mateusz Klich were withdrawn at half time. They were replaced by Pascal Struijk and Jamie Shackleton, but just as many balls seemed to be given away in midfield.

The Whites carried on though and Raphinha was desperately unlucky to see De Gea somehow claw away his fine volley. From the resultant corner, Manchester United broke away and JAMES (66) gave Luke Ayling the slip, before planting the ball in the net via Illan Meslier's open legs.

Shortly afterwards, Martial fell down in the penalty area to a clumsy challenge from Pascal Struijk. FERNANDES (70) made no mistake and rolled in the spot kick which followed. The Whites managed to keep out any more goals and DALLAS (73) scored with a fine effort into De Gea's top corner.

Bielsa's men carried on, urged on by their animated coach. Bamford and Harrison had shots blocked before the Manchester City loanee sent another effort just the wrong side of the post.

Over the years we've witnessed games where we felt much more upset than after this one. Matches in which we were robbed, cheated or undeservedly beaten. The emotions felt after this game were very hard to describe, but not nearly as painful as might have been expected from such a rinsing.

League Position: 14th

"The chances created in the first half were similar in the amount of opportunities. The difference in the first half was that they took their chances and we didn't. The way that both teams attacked was different. They took advantage of our misplaced passing when we tried to build the attack and this is how they created the majority of their chances.

When we were in our attacks, our return was not as quick as their transmission from the attack. It is very difficult to take. We're very sad and we regret that we weren't able to make more of the game.

In this or in any game there is always an obligation to try to win the next game. Of course, when we lose, there are questions about the style of play and when we win we are praised for it. We will try to improve all of the things that came up as a difficulty in this game."

-Marcelo Bielsa

In the forty-one minutes of the press conference, Bielsa went into great detail about his philosophies and it was difficult to disagree with anything that he said. Of course, the news hounds widely misquoted the United coach.

The exotically named Etienne Fermie claimed in The Sun that Bielsa had said that United were superior to the Red Devils. A similar claim was also made by Jonathan Spencer in the Daily Mail. Gary Lineker even piled in with a sarcastic comment that United are really fun to watch, but even more fun to play against.

The ladies and gentlemen of the media never take it too well when one of their targets bites back at them. Bielsa's resentment about some of the comments came from his belief that the press were seeking to upset his players.

To the admiration of practically every United fan, he made the point very clearly that he would not be causing confusion amongst his young team by altering his tactics.

He defends his players and philosophy but never himself and throughout his time at Elland Road, he has never proffered a single excuse for any reason whatsoever. United now returned to the serious business of seeking to take points away from teams who were positioned lower than them in the table.

Burnley were competing in their fourth consecutive Premier League campaign and finished tenth in the 2019-20 season. Their manager, Sean Dyche, was highly regarded and the Clarets were seen as a financially steady club who were probably punching above their weight.

Burnley's style though, was dour and completely the opposite to Bielsa's approach. They scored their goals usually from set pieces and breakaways, so it was unlikely that an attractive game would arise.

Leeds United 1-0 Burnley
27th December, 2020

Leeds United
Meslier, Ayling, Phillips, Struijk, Dallas, Klich (Shackleton 66), Alioski, Raphinha (Poveda 70), Rodrigo (Hernandez 59), Harrison, Bamford.

Burnley
Pope, Lowton, Tarkowski, Mee, Taylor, Benson (Stephens 74), Brownhill, Westwood, Pieters (Rodriguez 74), Wood, Barnes.

Referee: Robert Jones

Two former United favourites lined up for Burnley. Chris Wood and Charlie Taylor had joined the Clarets in darker days when the Whites were most definitely a selling club. This was a reminder of how far United had come since Bielsa took charge.

With Koch, Llorente and Cooper injured, the Whites once again fielded a makeshift defence and this gave some cause for concern, given Burnley's strength at set pieces.

Luke Ayling pumped the ball over the heads of the Burnley defence and as Patrick Bamford raced after it, the striker found himself with only the Burnley keeper to beat. As Bamford prepared to skip around him, Nick Pope unceremoniously dumped the United man on to the deck.

Robert Jones pointed to the spot and BAMFORD (5) smashed it into the net. It was good to see him scoring a penalty in such a manner. There was none of the languid, casual approach that we have seen in the past, but the actions of a striker who is full of confidence and at the top of his game.

Bamford admitted after the match that he had been given the heads up to take the penalty by Mateusz Klich, after the Pole's first weak effort against West Ham United. Shortly afterwards, Burnley were involved in a penalty claim of their own. Ben Mee backed into Illan Meslier, who rose much higher than him and as the ball came loose, Ashley Barnes shot it into the empty net.

Mee was judged to have fouled the Frenchman and the general opinion was that United had got away with it. Then Raphinha and Jack Harrison both came close for the Whites, with the latter being particularly unlucky when Patrick Bamford somehow got in the way of his shot.

Too many United attacks were breaking down as Burnley sat back and soaked up the pressure, while at the other end, Chris Wood headed over the bar after being well policed by Luke Ayling.

In the second half, Burnley picked themselves up and battered the home defence, throwing absolutely everything at them. Kalvin Phillips was doing his impression of 'spring heeled Jack' as he rose to meet every challenge in all four corners of the penalty area.

Illan Meslier and Luke Ayling also starred in the rearguard action as the Whites repelled attack after attack. For a team that was statistically weak at set pieces, United were doing very well.

As the clock ran down, Nick Pope left his goal and appeared in the attacking box for every Burnley corner and suitable free kick.

Like a good horror movie, it was both thrilling and frightening to watch and when the final whistle was blown, everybody in white released a great sigh of relief.

More noted for their attacking prowess, the Whites showed that they could also defend when required to do so. Needless to say, Sean Dyche spent all his time moaning about the disallowed goal and did not pay his opponents any compliments at all.

League Position: 12th

"In the first half, we defended very well. This was helped by the fact we finished our attacks in the opposing half. In the second half, we had to defend closer to our own goal. It was difficult to solve some duels, especially in the last part of the game.

It was an energetic and valiant effort by the guys and very decisive. Our objective was to compete on an even keel with all our opponents in the Premier League but it's not an easy task.

For example, if you look at what happened at the end of the second half. We had to adapt to a situation which we hadn't faced up until now and where the result was in danger. Every game in the Premier League is a big challenge."

-Marcelo Bielsa

On 16th December, Slaven Bilic was sacked by West Bromwich Albion despite achieving promotion in the previous season. The current campaign was a disaster for him and his team though, despite credible draws against Chelsea and Manchester City, in his final game.

Having said that, the Baggies found themselves in nineteenth position having amassed only eleven points. Nevertheless, many people felt that the decision to dismiss him was harsh, but it only served to remind everyone of the cut-throat nature of the Premier League and football in general. He was replaced by Sam Allardyce, who had 'done the rounds' and stayed out of football management since his sacking from Everton in May 2018.

Following a heavy home defeat to Aston Villa in Allardyce's first game in charge, the Baggies then earned a draw at Anfield. The optimists saw this as the possible beginning of the fabled 'new manager bounce' and looked for better things when the Hawthorns side took on Leeds United.

As it proved, a 'dead cat bounce' was more fitting.

West Bromwich Albion 0-5 Leeds United
29th December, 2020

West Bromwich Albion
Johnstone, Furlong, Ajayi, O'Shea, Peltier, Sawyers, Phillips (Ivanovic 45), Gallagher, Grant (Pereira 61), Diangana (Krovinovic 72), Robinson.

Leeds United
Meslier, Dallas, Ayling, Struijk, Alioski, Phillips, Raphinha (Costa 81), Rodrigo (Hernandez 70), Klich (Shackleton 58), Harrison, Bamford.

Referee: Lee Mason

United received a unexpected late Christmas gift from the home side and SAWYERS (9) was the donor. Under no pressure whatsoever, he passed the ball back to his goalkeeper from twenty-five yards without looking up. Sam Johnstone was not where Romaine Sawyers imagined him to be and the ball rolled into an empty net.

Not needing any further encouragement, the Whites mounted attack after attack. Just over twenty minutes after the opener, ALIOSKI (31) raced down the left and smashed one of his 'specials' across the goal, into the top right hand corner.

In a blistering nine minute spell, HARRISON (36) was next to join the party. He enacted a fine exchange with Patrick Bamford, before getting the ball on to his left foot and firing it home. Then, following good work from Mateusz Klich, RODRIGO (40) deflected the ball into the net for number four.

Although United kept up the pressure in the second half, they found that goals were not quite as easy to come by. In fact, the Baggies nearly scored a goal of their own.

Klich, who was clearly struggling with an injury, sent a back pass to Illan Meslier who promptly presented the ball to Diangana. However, the young Frenchman redeemed himself with a fine save from the shot that followed.

The Pole was replaced by Jamie Shackleton, who deputised with his usual reliability. The youngster was soon involved in an eye catching give-and-go with Stuart Dallas. The Irishman then fed the ball to RAPHINHA (72), who gratefully curled a fine shot into the top corner.

In his usual way, Bielsa urged his men forward again and in the end, the home side could have counted themselves lucky not to have conceded more goals. This game clearly showed the difference in class between the two promoted sides.

League Position: 11th

"The team was very efficient, from eight chances, we managed to score five goals, even if one wasn't through our own doing. Normally, from eight chances, we score a maximum of two goals, so with such efficiency, the win margin was much higher.

Apart from that, I think we defended well and didn't commit any avoidable errors. Every game in this league is a challenge, because all the teams have secret capacities and all the teams present a different challenge.

For us, we've only been in this league for sixteen games and there are still many challenges and many tests that we have to pass before we can legitimately say that we belong."

-Marcelo Bielsa

Amazon Prime covered the match against West Bromwich Albion and former England international, Karen Carney, was one of the pundits. From a couple of statements made, she certainly did not endear herself to the United fans or club officials!

Firstly, she trotted out the old chestnut suggesting that the Whites were likely to burn themselves out in the Premier League. She then offered the outrageous and offensive opinion that the only reason this didn't happen during United's promotion campaign was due to the break brought about by the COVID-19 pandemic.

Unsurprisingly, there was a massive outcry on social media and sadly, a small amount of this was offensive, as well as sexist. Andrea Radrizzani later condemned Carney's statements but in the media the following day, several journalists suggested that the offensive stuff was drummed up by the Club.

This, of course, was almost as inaccurate and offensive as Carney's own remarks. Radrizzani later condemned the abuse, but thankfully did not retract his statement. It is to be hoped that in future, Ms. Carney spends a little more time on her research and thinks carefully before making offensive remarks herself.

Chapter Four
Reality Returns

Although I have never had the pleasure of visiting Tottenham Hotspur's fine new stadium, I have of course visited their former home of White Hart Lane on many occasions. Probably the most bizarre occasion was in September 1998.

White Hart Lane was one of the grounds that I preferred to drive to because the rail and tube connections were and still are a bit of a pain.

In those days, my favoured method was to drive down to the Haringey Irish Centre on Pretoria Road. It was easy enough to nip down the A10, turn off at The North Middlesex Hospital and park securely at the centre.

Apart from the excellent Guinness, the centre provided an unlimited supply of free sandwiches for anybody who had paid a fiver to use their car park. This arrangement was much better than going to the hot dog stall in front of the ground and buying a burger from the man with dirty fingernails.

The Irish centre was a friendly place and always a hive of activity, but sadly closed its doors for the last time in July 2020.

George Graham was the United manager, after taking over from Howard Wilkinson in 1996, when it became clear that the manager of the First Division champions had lost his way.

Graham had been a highly successful player and manager for Arsenal. As manager, his teams were First Division champions in 1989 and 1991, FA Cup winners in 1993, as well as League Cup winners in 1987 and 1993. They even lifted the European Cup Winners Cup trophy in 1994.

His career with Arsenal ended in ignominy however when he admitted receiving an 'unsolicited payment' from Rune Hauge, a Norwegian football agent. To make matters worse, he was banned for twelve months by the Football League.

Having served his ban, Graham came in and steadied the ship with his unattractive but effective brand of defensive football. Nevertheless, there were persistent rumours about both his personal life as well as his health.

By the time that the Spurs game was about to take place, several reports appeared in the media that he was anxious to return to London and that his destination was likely to be White Hart Lane.

What made this match unique in my mind was the way that both the United and Spurs fans joined together in perfect harmony to chant and shout abuse at Graham.

The fans who had travelled from West Yorkshire saw his impending defection as a betrayal, whilst their North London counterparts just couldn't stomach the fact that they were about to be managed by the man who had brought such success to their hated local rivals.

The game was an exciting one and swung backwards and forwards with Gunnar Halle, Jimmy Floyd-Hasselbaink and Clyde Wijnhard scoring for the Whites.

Ramon Vega, Steffen Iversen and Sol Campbell scored for the home side.

Midway through the following week, Tottenham Hotspur duly appointed George Graham as manager, which then saw David O'Leary step up and take the manager's job at Elland Road.

The likeable, if lightweight Irishman had been mentored by Graham. O'Leary was very fortunate to walk into a virtuous circle of a confident team that was starting to be augmented by the most promising group of young players that the club had produced since the days of Don Revie.

Between O'Leary's appointment and his dismissal in 2001, United enjoyed their last golden era. They were consistently around the top five of the Premier League and acquitted themselves well in the Champions League without winning anything.

As we know, things rapidly went sour and thanks to the Ponzi-like dealings of Peter Ridsdale and his board, United became and remain the highest profile casualty of financial mismanagement in English football.

Tottenham Hotspur 3-0 Leeds United
2nd January, 2021

Tottenham Hotspur
Lloris, Doherty, Alderweireld, Dier, Davies, Winks (Sissoko 76), Hojbjerg, Bergwijn, Ndombele (Moura 78), Son, Kane (Vinicius 87).

Leeds United
Meslier, Dallas, Ayling, Struijk, Alioski (Shackleton 64), Phillips, Raphinha, Rodrigo (Hernandez 65), Klich, Harrison (Poveda 61), Bamford.

Referee: David Coote

Spurs have one of the finest new stadiums in Europe and unquestionably the finest striking partnership. Harry Kane and Son Heung-min are fine players in their own right, but as a combination they are lethal.

Whilst United approached this match without fear, it was a fundamental mistake that led to the first goal. Illan Meslier is normally one of the best distributors of the ball in the Premier League, but his sloppy pass was picked up by Winks who passed to Bergwijn who was upended by Gjanni Alioski.

Although the infringement appeared to have taken place outside the box, the VAR confirmed that it wasn't and referee Coote pointed to the spot. KANE (29) stepped up and dispatched the penalty with his usual confidence.

Up to that point, the attacking honours were about even with Bamford coming close for United twice and Kane threatening for the London side.

Spurs' next goal was a fine effort which showcased the talents of both Kane and Son. The England striker found his partner with a defence-splitting pass and SON (43) completed the move in style.

United kept battling but were dealt a killer blow early in the second half as ALDERWEIRELD (50) rose above Kalvin Phillips and Patrick Bamford to head the ball home.

The Whites kept plugging away, but Spurs were now content to sit back and soak up the pressure as United's attempts became increasingly ragged.

League Position: 12th

"The first thirty minutes was positive. The final fifteen minutes of the first half were slightly more even and the first fifteen minutes of the second half was the most difficult moment, when they were better than us.

In the game we created ten chances and didn't score and our opponents created twelve and scored three. For me, the difference was of course the efficiency and the fact that their offensive game came about through errors that we could have avoided.

I think the capacity for our forwards to unbalance their defence was sufficient and our capacity to defend was also good. We had possibilities to unbalance in attack and showed that we can defend against some top forwards."

-Marcelo Bielsa

The third round of the FA Cup used to be eagerly awaited and though this competition has not been devalued as much as the League Cup, it carries only a fraction of its former importance.

Many fans were hoping for a modest cup run for a change, but it seemed that Marcelo Bielsa did not see it that way.

Most fans and pundits felt that United had already done enough to indicate that they would not be involved in a relegation struggle.

The man from Rosario did not agree. The tunnel vision and focus that he has been famous for came in to play to ensure that he would not be making any assumptions until safety was assured in a mathematical sense.

Almost contrary to this, fans were relieved when he announced a fairly strong side which included Liam Cooper who was returning from injury.

Crawley Town 3-0 Leeds United
10th January, 2021

Crawley Town
Morris, Francomb, Tunnicliffe, Craig, Dallison (M. Wright 90), Matthews (Davies 71), Hessenthaler (Doherty 90), Powell, Tsaroulla (J. Wright 72), Nadesan (Watters 72), Nichols.

Leeds United
Casilla, Phillips, Cooper (Casey 45), Davis (Raphinha 58), Struijk (Jenkins 45), Shackleton, Alioski, Hernandez, Poveda (Greenwood 58), Rodrigo (Harrison 45), Costa.

Referee: Peter Bankes

Up until half time there were a lot of positives. A strong starting eleven had been selected, Rodrigo had a legitimate penalty claim and Casilla had made a decent stop. Kalvin Phillips was given an airing because his forthcoming one match suspension did not apply to the FA Cup and Liam Cooper was finding his feet after a recent injury.

When Cooper was removed at the interval, it came as no surprise. What was surprising was the rest of the changes and those that happened subsequently.

It was simply one change too many. Jack Harrison was not convincing in the role of lone striker instead of Rodrigo. Removing Struijk as well as Cooper, also put an unnecessary strain on the defence. Although Jenkins and Casey worked hard, the disruption was just too much for them. Of course, when Raphinha and the youngster Sam Greenwood came on, the damage was already done.

Crawley Manager, John Yems, could not believe his luck when five minutes into the second half, goalkeeper Glen Morris found speedy winger TSAROULLA (50) who beat Shackleton, Hernandez and Casey before slotting the ball into the top right hand corner.

The Whites looked rattled and when Leif Davis tried to find Jack Harrison, the makeshift striker could not hold on to the ball and Nichols was able to find NADESAN (53), who beat the exposed Casilla a little too easily.

United were all over the place and this was not helped by the introduction of Raphinha and Greenwood for Poveda and Davis. Phillips, who had moved to the centre of defence fouled Nadesan, who took the free kick himself. Casilla couldn't clear the ball properly and it fell to TUNNICLIFFE (70) who smashed it into the roof of the net.

Crawley Town then added insult to injury by giving a three minute run out to Mark Wright, the reality television performer and has-been footballer.

"In the first half, we played better than the opponent and the game was played how we wanted it to be played, even if we didn't create much danger. In the second half, the game was played how the opponents wanted to play and they did create danger to deserve the goals which they scored. The result generates a lot of sadness and disappointment for us."

-Marcelo Bielsa

Nearly a week later, United were at home to another Sussex club and were widely expected to pick up all three points against Brighton & Hove Albion. Kiko Casilla started in goal as Illan Meslier was unavailable due to illness and Kalvin Phillips was also missing due to his one match suspension.

Leeds United 0-1 Brighton & Hove Albion
16th January, 2021

Leeds United
Casilla, Dallas, Ayling, Cooper, Alioski (Hernandez 67), Struijk, Harrison, Rodrigo (Roberts 62), Klich, Raphinha (Poveda 75), Bamford.

Brighton & Hove Albion
Sanchez, Webster, Dunk, Burn, Veltman, White, Gross, March, Trossard (Tau 73), Mac Allister (Bissouma 62), Maupay (Propper 81).

Referee: Kevin Friend

This game was an unusually mediocre performance from the Whites. The Elland Road pitch was in the worst condition that most of us have seen it in many years. The bumps, lumps and piles of mud were due to a combination of the appalling weather and the fact that the normal end of season maintenance had not taken place, owing to the lack of time available.

The Whites started sluggishly and just couldn't seem to get going and were even driven to lofting long balls up to Patrick Bamford. When a slick passing move did appear, it came from the visitors and ended up with MAUPAY (17) tapping the ball into the net, having given Luke Ayling the slip.

Rodrigo came closest for United, but he failed to connect properly with an Alioski cross. Trossard hit the top side of the post with a deflected effort before half time.

Just after the hour mark, the introduction of Pablo Hernandez and Tyler Roberts brightened things up a bit but it was already clear that this was going to be one of those frustrating days when the Whites were going to come away empty handed.

Jack Harrison was the standout player for United and it goes without saying that former favourite, Ben White, had a very good game for the Seagulls.

League Position: 12th

"I think we defended below our capabilities, below our usual level. We only managed to recover the ball close to our own goal.

Every time we lost the ball, the adaptations took us to the edge of our own area to recover the ball. We attacked below our usual capabilities.

We didn't attack well and we also didn't defend well either and we also didn't play well, but the result could still have been different. Even whilst playing below our capabilities we could have aspired to a better result."

-Marcelo Bielsa

Chapter Five
Midway Matches

Trips to Newcastle over the years have usually been good fun whatever the result, with a pint in either the Strawberry Pub or the long-vanished Federation Social Club. 'The Fed' as it was universally known was owned by the Northern Clubs Federation Brewery in Gateshead.

This was an interesting business which was a co-operative venture and produced beer almost exclusively for the North East working mens clubs from 1921, until the Brewery was acquired by S&N (later Heineken) in 2004.

It was a very successful business in its heyday and the beers were of good quality and usually slightly cheaper than anything else on the market.
One of the most memorable trips was in the season 1966 and remains the only time that I have attended a match on Christmas Eve.

This was quite commonplace in those days, especially if the day fell on a Saturday. In fact it was only ten years earlier that United played their final Christmas Day fixture. In 1966, we didn't have time for a pint as the coach only arrived at St. James Park in time for the three o'clock kick off.

It was a tight game, but the Whites managed to edge a win by two goals to one. The scorers on the day were Mike O'Grady and Albert Johanneson.

My copy of the programme from St. James' Park, collected on Christmas Eve in 1966.

When we arrived back in Yorkshire, we repaired straight away to my good friend Roger Goldthorpe's house. I was employed by Tetley's at the time and I had managed to get Roger a firkin (nine gallons) of mild beer at a good discount.

I had tapped the cask a couple of days earlier and Roger was under strict instructions not to pour any until Christmas Eve. Roger was true to his word and the beer was perfect. The assembled company then proceeded to enjoy every last drop of it.

Two days later on Boxing Day 1966, the Magpies played the return match at Elland Road. The Whites murdered them 5-0 in front of a crowd of over 40,000. Peter Lorimer bagged two of the goals and the other three were shared between Jack Charlton, Jim Storrie and Terry Cooper.

Newcastle United 1-2 Leeds United
26th, January 2021

Newcastle United
Darlow, Hayden, Lascelles, Schar, Lewis, Murphy (Saint-Maximin 64), Shelvey, Hendrick, Almiron, Fraser (Gayle 77), Wilson.

Leeds United
Meslier, Ayling, Llorente (Struijk 10), Cooper, Alioski (Klich 56), Phillips, Raphinha, Dallas Rodrigo, Harrison, Bamford (Roberts 60).

Referee: Anthony Taylor

Summer signing, Diego Llorente, lined up for his first appearance of 2021 only to break down after ten minutes with a muscle strain. He was replaced by Pascal Struijk, who was able to return to his preferred role in the centre of defence.

United soon got going and Jack Harrison sliced a volley, but it was notable that both of the visitors' wide men were going to cause the Magpies a few problems.

Raphinha was popping up all over the place and Rodrigo set him up after good work from Gjanni Alioski and Patrick Bamford. RAPHINHA (17) coolly put the ball beyond Darlow's reach.

Shortly afterwards, the Brazilian rapped another shot to the outside of the post, having been set up again by Rodrigo. This could have put the Whites out of sight, but instead Newcastle came back early in the second half.

Patrick Bamford and Luke Ayling got caught in possession, allowing Callum Wilson and Miguel Almiron to play a quick exchange, leaving the impressive ALMIRON (57) to race through and level the scores.

This event seemed to galvanise the Whites and Raphinha picked out a beautiful cross to HARRISON (61). This time, the Manchester City loanee sent a powerful rising volley into the right hand corner.

The game then swung from end-to-end with Alain Saint-Maximin and Jonjo Shelvey being the main protagonists. Both keepers were up to their tasks however and the Whites deservedly won.

League Position: 12th

"There were moments where we played well. There were moments when we didn't play badly and moments when we played badly. In the moments that we didn't play well, the game was neutral.

In the twenty minutes where we played badly, which was after the Harrison goal we put the result in danger. Probably, the result was deserved but those twenty minutes put Newcastle in a position where they could have drawn the game.

It was important for us to win. The majority of teams go on runs similar to the ones that we've had and they are also longer and more difficult. So the quicker that you get out of these runs, the better."

-Marcelo Bielsa

Five days later, United faced Leicester City at the King Power Stadium. Because of the way that the Foxes had taken the Whites apart at Elland Road, few people fancied United for more than a point. Star striker, Jamie Vardy, was not available but the form of the Brendan Rogers' side did not seem to be affected having been unbeaten in their last seven going in to this encounter.

Leicester City 1-3 Leeds United
31st January, 2021

Leicester City
Schmeichel, Castagne (Pereira 36), Fofana (Under 80), Evans, Justin, Tielemans, Mendy, Albrighton (Soyuncu 45), Maddison, Barnes, Perez.

Leeds United
Meslier, Ayling, Struijk, Cooper, Alioski, Phillips, Raphinha (Costa 80), Rodrigo (Klich 21), Dallas, Harrison, Bamford.

Referee: Chris Kavanagh

After only thirteen minutes, a really fluid movement produced the first goal of the game. James Maddison exchanged a neat one-two with BARNES (13), who dispatched the ball confidently past the exposed Meslier. In view of what happened the last time that the two sides had met, there was an uneasy feeling that history was about to repeat itself.

United were having none of this however, and within two minutes, Luke Ayling had intercepted a through ball. 'Bill' found Patrick Bamford, who in turn picked out DALLAS (15) and the Cookstown man timed his run perfectly to smash it into the net.

Not long after United's equaliser, Rodrigo stretched too far giving himself what looked like a serious groin strain. He was replaced by Mateusz Klich.

Both sides then had VAR judgements go against them. First, the home team had a shot disallowed for offside and United suffered the same fate, as their former keeper Schmeichel clawed Patrick Bamford's header from under the bar and presented Mateusz Klich with an easy chance. Sadly, the Pole was judged to be offside.

Harrison and Raphinha both came close before half time, but the Leicester keeper was once again showing his class as the two sides left the pitch after an exciting and entertaining first half. The Foxes switched to a 3-4-3 formation after the break and started the second half looking more solid.

With twenty minutes to go, Pascal Struijk beat Perez to the ball and found Raphinha, who sent a perfect through ball to BAMFORD (70). United's number nine had time to let the ball run to his trusty left foot before unleashing an unstoppable shot into the top corner of the net.

Leicester fought back and put the Whites under all sorts of pressure, before the men from Yorkshire wrapped the game up with one of their trademark breakaways.

Stuart Dallas got to the ball before Mendy and sent Klich away down the left flank. The Pole found Patrick Bamford, who accelerated his run and unselfishly left HARRISON (84) with the simple task of completing a truly wonderful move.

This was an impressive and deserved win for the Whites. With Rodrigo being substituted on twenty-one minutes and Raphinha on eighty minutes, this meant that the United team which finished the match solely consisted of players who had performed in the Championship the season before.

League Position: 12th

"It was a very difficult game. In the first half the game was how we expected. In the second half, they changed the distribution of their players. It took us about ten minutes to adjust to this. After, we started to recover better and scored the second goal.

After our second goal, it was the most difficult period for about ten minutes. We couldn't prevent them from creating goalscoring opportunities. At the end of the game, we managed it well. It was a difficult result for us to achieve.

The only way that we could be better than them was not to allow them to build up passes. In the Championship, we played to be the best. At this level, we have to make a massive effort to be able to keep up, to look like our opponents, to not let them be superior to us. But when the club decided to build the squad for this campaign, all the players that were conserved, they were conserved because we thought they could live up to the expectations of playing in this league."

-Marcelo Bielsa

Leeds United 1-2 Everton
3rd February, 2021

Leeds United
Meslier, Ayling, Struijk, Cooper, Alioski
(Hernandez 78), Phillips, Raphinha, Klich (Roberts
69), Dallas, Harrison (Costa 87), Bamford.

Everton
Olsen, Holgate, Mina, Godfrey, Digne, Doucoure,
Gomes, Iwobi (King 87), Sigurdsson (Davies 89),
Richarlison (Keane 80), Calvert-Lewin.

Referee: Michael Oliver

The most important debut in this match was the
pitch. It was United's only 'signing' in the January
transfer window and came courtesy of Tottenham
Hotspur for a fee of £300,000.

The badly cut up surface was starting to cause
United problems and was more suited to the hit and
hope style of play than the fast passing game
favoured by the Whites. The relaying of the pitch in
February was a temporary measure until the end of
the season.

Players of both sides were struggling to keep their
feet on the slick surface, but it was a massive
improvement on what had gone before.
The Toffees took an early lead, as Digne waltzed
through the United defence before crossing to
SIGURDSSON (16) who gleefully buried his shot.

United started to fight back and Mateusz Klich forced a fine save out of Robin Olsen. This effort was followed by Patrick Bamford heading a chance over the bar.

Both Raphinha and Kalvin Phillips took good quality free kicks not long after. The Brazilian found Gjanni Alioski who hit a rasping volley against the post. Phillips found Pascal Struijk, who forced another fine save from Olsen.

The Whites found themselves on the receiving end of a corner taken which Ben Godfrey picked up at the near post. The defender then flicked it across to CALVERT-LEWIN (41) who crashed (with the ball) into the back of the net.

Goals just before half time are never welcomed by the recipients, but United made a timely and positive response. At the beginning of the second period, they immediately took the game to Everton. Patrick Bamford prodded the ball to RAPHINHA (48) who found the back of the net with a low shot.

As the Whites continued to apply the pressure, Robin Olsen was having the game of his life, using this rare opportunity to show off his considerable prowess. The Everton reserve goalkeeper then made fine saves from Klich, Raphinha and Harrison as the pressure mounted.

Everton had a penalty shout when the ball hit Luke Ayling's arm, but VAR judged it to be accidental.

As the clock ran down, Everton attempted to shut up shop and dangerous forays from United were few and far between. Nevertheless, they nearly equalised in the dying minutes. Raphinha sent a beautiful ball to Patrick Bamford, who in turn set up Tyler Roberts. Although the Wales international had time to kill the ball, his shot was badly sliced and that was that.

League Position: 11th

"In the first thirty minutes, we played well and we created danger proportional to the dominance that we had. It's true that in the final fifteen minutes of the first half, we didn't create many goalscoring opportunities.

Our idea was to avoid their third goal because if they had scored a third, it would've been very difficult to get back into the game.

It was very important to defend well, thinking that if we continued our attacking performance, that we would reduce the margin. While it happened this way, we couldn't create any of the chances that we created into the second goal.

Our offensive game was enough for us to think we could have scored with the chances we had. Normally we would score two or three goals."

-Marcelo Bielsa

The next match was Crystal Palace, at Elland Road. Many people felt that the corresponding game at Selhurst Park was a bit of a fluke and that Palace were unworthy of the 4-1 scoreline. This encounter then was the ideal opportunity for revenge.

Leeds United 2-0 Crystal Palace
8th February, 2021

Leeds United
Meslier, Ayling, Struijk, Cooper, Alioski, Phillips (Shackleton 88), Raphinha, Dallas, Klich, Harrison, Bamford.

Crystal Palace
Guaita, Clyne, Dann, Cahill, Mitchell, Eze, Milivojevic, Riedewald, van Aanholt (Townsend 45), Mateta (Batshuayi 65), Ayew (Benteke 76).

Referee: Andre Marriner

United started purposefully and within three minutes, they were ahead. Stuart Dallas found HARRISON (3), who sent a right footed shot which was deflected into the net by Gary Cahill.

The former Chelsea man was having a nightmare. He was dispossessed by Patrick Bamford who wasted a golden opportunity to finish.

Worse was to come as he was nutmegged by Raphinha, before fouling the Brazilian out of sheer desperation.

It was almost a penalty, but Raphinha set Struijk up with the free kick and the Dutchman couldn't direct his header.

Early in the second half, Raphinha was in the thick of it again. He picked up Mateusz Klich's pass and sent in a good shot which Guaita could only parry away to the feet of BAMFORD (52), whose tenacity was rewarded with a simple tap in.

Bamford came close a couple more times, but Jack Harrison came closest when he rattled the crossbar. This was a result which was much more comprehensive than the scoreline suggests and justice had been done.

League Position: 10th

"I think the fact that we didn't concede any goals was important. We didn't suffer any chances in the first half and very few in the second.

Although in the end we didn't attack as much, throughout the game, we generally caused them danger.

The fact that we won the Championship is always more distant, further away. We are taking our step into the Premier League now by trying to play as naturally as possible and to show that we deserve to be in this league."

-Marcelo Bielsa

Chapter Six
Faded Fortunes

Back in 1966, I was working at Tetley's Brewery in Leeds and like many of my contemporaries at work, I was part of a syndicate on the football pools. I paid my shilling every week and usually thought no more about it. One particular week was different, when our organiser had managed to pick seven draws on the coupon.

Only one person, an office cleaner in London had managed to pick eight draws and she won the first dividend which amounted to £60,000. In today's money that figure was worth around £1 million.

Our second dividend was worth £90 each and as I earned about £10 per week in those days, it was very welcome. A good friend of mine, Brian Rogers was also in the syndicate and we looked for a way to spend the money as quickly as possible.

Brian lived a stone's throw from Elland Road and of course he was a United fan. The Whites were away to Arsenal on November 5th and the following Monday, they were away to West Ham in the League Cup.

We each took a couple of days of holiday and arranged a trip to London to watch both matches.

We took the train down on the Saturday morning and checked into the Great Northern Hotel. Our first port of call was the Rising Sun (now The Rocket) on Euston Road. This pub was the obligatory first stop for all Leeds people in the 1960s and 70s.

There was good reason for this because as well as being close to Kings Cross station, it was one of the few Tetley's pubs in the capital at that time. There was just time for another quick pint in The Woodbine at Highbury before the match.

This pub has been in Irish hands since 1919 and still has a traditional interior nowadays, but on a recent visit, I failed to spot the nicotine-stained photos of the Cork hurlers.

The Woodbine Pub, North London, in the modern day.

Like many clashes with the Gunners in those days, this was a very close encounter with Jack Charlton scoring the only goal of the game.

We started on the beer a little bit early on the Monday morning, given that the kick off against West Ham was not until 7.30pm. By the time we staggered out of the Boleyn Tavern at 7.15pm, we were not in the best of order.

I cannot remember a single detail about this match, which is rather as well because the Hammers ran out 7-0 winners. I did discover that the United team was the same side that had beaten Arsenal two days earlier and so it is better that a veil is drawn over this particular memory!

By the Tuesday morning, we had almost run out of money and so it was time to return home. Another thing that I cannot remember was why we didn't think to purchase return tickets on the train. Hitch hiking was then the only alternative if we were to get home in time for work on the following day.

We took a bus out as far as Hatfield and eventually managed to get a ride on a lorry as far as the Ram Jam Inn near Oakham on the A1. Eventually, we saw a prosperous looking gentleman leave the pub. As he started to fumble with his car keys, we asked him if he could give us a lift North. Although he initially said that he was only going as far as Newark, he soon admitted that he was going to Newcastle.

He explained in the car that his first impressions of us were not positive and thought that we might have robbed him or stolen his car.

As the journey progressed, he became more friendly and our only concern was the half bottle of whiskey that he kept swigging. By way of explanation, he said that the whiskey helped to keep him awake!

The lift was a good result and we were very thankful when he dropped us at the Boot and Shoe at Peckfield. From there, we were able to walk into Kippax and get a bus into Leeds.

There's an old saying that;
"Stupid young fools make the best of old men."
The first part of the proverb definitely applies to me, but I'm still trying to become a decent old man!

Arsenal 4-2 Leeds United
14th February, 2021

Arsenal
Leno, Bellerin, Luiz, Gabriel, Soares, Ceballos (Holding 89), Xhaka, Saka, Odegaard (Elneny 78), Smith-Rowe (Willian 62), Aubameyang.

Leeds United
Meslier, Shackleton, Ayling, Cooper, Alioski (Huggins 53), Struijk, Raphinha, Dallas, Klich (Roberts 45), Harrison (Costa 45), Bamford.

Referee: Stuart Attwell

From the start, United struggled to handle Arsenal's high press. Getting out of their own half, proved to be a struggle for the Whites. AUBAMEYANG (13) took full advantage of the situation, intercepting a Meslier pass and shooting into the corner of the net.

Not long after, Stuart Attwell awarded a penalty against Liam Cooper, but VAR adjudged that Saka was already on his way down before contact was made.

Moments later, Saka was awarded another penalty. Illan Meslier was really struggling with the Arsenal press and held on to the ball for too long.

As he desperately attempted to clear, he brought Bukayo Saka down. AUBAMEYANG (41) made no mistake with the penalty.

He rarely does. Fired up by his two goals, the French striker then found BELLERIN (45+2) at the far post to compound United's misery.

United introduced Helder Costa and Tyler Roberts to start the second half, but Costa was caught napping by Emile Smith-Rowe who dispossessed him.

The young forward found AUBAMEYANG (47) who nodded in a neat header at the far post to complete his hat-trick.

Niall Huggins made his debut for Leeds, replacing Gjanni Alioski. The thrill that the youngster must have experienced was only tempered by the scoreline.

However heavily they are being beaten, this United side do not let their heads drop and STRUIJK (58) rose above the Arsenal defence to smash home a bullet header.

Eleven minutes later, United reduced the deficit further. Tyler Roberts pulled a neat pass back from the dead ball line for COSTA (69) to slot home.

A Tyler Roberts back heel then sent Patrick Bamford through, but the striker was sandwiched between two defenders. The Whites were unlucky not to be awarded a penalty for this, but such is life.

League Position: 11th

"In the first half, we didn't manage to break the circulation of Arsenal from their half to our half. When building up from the back we didn't manage to take the ball from our half to their half cleanly.

There was no surprise for either of the two managers. They knew how we were going to press and they resolved this. We knew how they would press but we didn't manage to resolve this. In the second half, the opposite happened."

-Marcelo Bielsa

Wolverhampton Wanderers 1-0 Leeds United
19th February, 2021

Wolverhampton Wanderers
Patricio, Dendoncker, Coady, Saiss, Semedo, Neves, Moutinho, Jonny (Marcal 60) (Ait-Nouri 82), Neto, Da Silva (Silva 87), Traore.

Leeds United
Meslier, Ayling, Struijk, Cooper, Dallas, Raphinha, Shackleton (Hernandez 66), Klich (Alioski 81), Harrison (Costa 81), Roberts, Bamford.

Referee: David Coote

It is a strange situation when a goalkeeper ends a game as man of the match and scores the only goal, by putting the ball into his own net. However, this is what happened in this game.

Despite the absence of Kalvin Phillips, the back line looked more composed than for a long time. Liam Cooper and Pascal Struijk bossed the centre of defence. Jamie Shackleton and Mateusz Klich shared the Phillips role and it seemed to be working.

The first half belonged to both defences, with real scoring opportunities being few and far between. Raphinha toiled away and a smart pass from the Brazilian allowed Mateusz Klich to fire a fine shot against the near post. Pascal Struijk followed up and this brought a fine save from Rui Patricio.

Three set pieces, one in the first half and two in the second were met by Liam Cooper and with any luck at all, he would have scored from at least one of those opportunities. Shortly afterwards, disaster struck for the Whites.

Adama Traore broke away, giving Pascal Struijk the slip. He then hit a shot which cannoned off the angle of the crossbar. The ball then struck the back of MESLIER (64), who was descending from an acrobatic leap and knew nothing about it until he was fishing it out from the back of the net.

United responded to the setback by laying siege to the Wolves goal. Patrick Bamford had the ball in the net, but he was adjudged to be marginally offside.

Costa and Raphinha also brought the best out of Rui Patricio, but it wasn't to be and the Whites had every reason to feel aggrieved that they were not even able to salvage a point.

League Position: 12th

"If you look back through the game, we dominated for the majority of it. There were very few periods when we weren't the dominant side. Look at the chances, we had double the chances that they did. We defended well, we attacked well, so this is the analysis that I have of the game at the moment."

-Marcelo Bielsa

Another Bielsa mural that turned up in Yorkshire. This time an outhouse in Menston, around thirty minutes from Elland Road.

Leeds United 3-0 Southampton
23rd February, 2021

Leeds United
Meslier, Llorente, Cooper, Struijk, Ayling, Klich (Alioski 59), Dallas, Harrison (Costa 45), Roberts (Hernandez 75), Raphinha, Bamford.

Southampton
McCarthy, Bednarek, Vestergaard, Salisu, Bertrand, Armstrong, Ward-Prowse, Romeu (Djenepo 70), Tella (Minamino 58), Adams, Redmond (Ings 58).

Referee: Andre Marriner

The relaid surface of the pitch was causing problems and the recent terrible weather conditions were not helping matters. Diego Llorente and Liam Cooper both slid around before getting their footing. United started on the front foot though with Tyler Roberts sending Patrick Bamford through, only for the striker to overhit the return ball.

It was Southampton who had the first real chance. The deadly accurate ball from James Ward-Prowse found the head of Jannik Vestergaard but Pascal Struijk did just enough to cause him to head the ball wide. Nathan Tella then literally gave Luke Ayling the slip, but shot the ball straight into the grateful arms of Illan Meslier.

Not long afterwards, Luke Ayling sent Raphinha away but his cutback was sent skyward by Tyler Roberts. The Brazilian then sent a great free kick across to Diego Llorente, who found Cooper, only for the captain to have his effort tipped over the bar by McCarthy.

Just before half time, the live wire Raphinha once again came close as he raced after a great through ball from Stuart Dallas. His effort was denied by a goal-saving tackle from Oriol Romeu.

Two minutes after the restart, Llorente found Tyler Roberts in the centre circle. The Wales international picked out BAMFORD (47) who smashed the ball clinically into the bottom corner from twenty yards.

Southampton had to open their game up, but although Stuart Armstrong tested Illan Meslier, the net result of their more open play was to let United in. McCarthy was having a busy time of it, parrying a Patrick Bamford shot as far as Tyler Roberts who shot it back at him.

At the other end, Che Adams chested the ball towards goal and from the resultant breakaway, Pablo Hernandez found Stuart Dallas who in turn played the ball to Helder Costa.

Costa then repaid the complement and DALLAS (78) toe poked the ball home for number two. RAPHINHA (84) took a magnificent free kick from twenty-five yards which dipped into the bottom corner of McCarthy's net.

The Brazilian removed his shirt to pay tribute to Ronaldinho's mother who had died earlier in the week. He was booked of course, but nobody begrudged him his emotional tribute.

By this time, Southampton were a spent force as Bielsa urged the Whites to keep on the attack. Pablo Hernandez came the closest but that was that. All in all, an efficient night's work for the Whites.

League Position: 10th

"In the second half, having been able to score so quickly, the game opened up.

The difference of three goals was bigger than the difference of the two teams. We had to put in a big effort not to allow them to dominate and an equally big effort to dominate them in the moments that we did.

Even if our offensive game was good, because we managed to create double the chances of the opponent the transmit of the game was alternate. The group that we have is, on the human aspect, the best thing about this experience.

All of those who have arrived have been protected and welcomed. The same goes for all the coaching staff, we also felt very welcome and integrated when we arrived."

-Marcelo Bielsa

Leeds United 0-1 Aston Villa
27th February, 2021

Leeds United
Meslier, Ayling, Llorente, Cooper, Dallas, Struijk (Alioski 53), Costa (Harrison 64), Roberts (Hernandez 71), Klich, Raphinha, Bamford.

Aston Villa
Martinez, El Mohamady, Konsa, Mings, Targett, McGinn, Nakamba, Ramsey (Sanson 79), Traore, Watkins, El Ghazi (Trezeguet 88).

Referee: Peter Bankes

Unlike their previous encounter with Villa, this one turned out to be a massively frustrating experience for United. Once again, the new surface was proving problematic for both teams. Only the music was missing from this version of the Skaters Waltz.

This manifested itself within the first minute when Patrick Bamford ended up on his backside and instead of making the net bulge, the ball skidded across goal to Raphinha at the far post. The Brazilian couldn't quite reach the ball and a great chance was missed.

At the other end, Ollie Watkins struck another mishit shot which found EL GHAZI (5), who made no mistake as Villa took an early lead.

As the first half wore on, United had the lion's share of possession but very few real chances to equalise. Raphinha continued to catch the eye with some mazy runs but more often than not, the final ball was not quite enough to cause a credible threat.

Long before the end of the first hour, it became clear that Villa were content to sit back and soak up the pressure.

After what happened to them in the corresponding fixture, when United ran riot, it was hard to blame the West Midlanders for taking this course. United just weren't themselves as Costa, Roberts and Klich all misfired.

Harrison replaced Costa and immediately sent a fine cross to Raphinha, but even our favourite Brazilian could not make the most of it. There were only a few positives to take from this game; mainly the defensive performances of Meslier, Llorente and Cooper. A game to forget and move on from.

League Position: 11th

"In the game, I think we played better than the opponent. We had many minutes of dominance, there were very few where we were dominated. In the first half, we created more chances than they did, even if they scored a goal.

The goal was a chance which was not intentional. A shot in which a player slips becomes a pass for a player who was not even asking for the ball. In general terms, we should have been ahead in the first half, given the chances that we had but we didn't defend as well in the first half as we did in the second.

In the second half, we defended very well. We had the ball for almost all of the half, but we created very little danger. The ball always finished in the opponent's box. We didn't concede any counter attacks. We lost the ball in the final third.

All of the crosses and passes from out wide into the centre were imprecise. In the set pieces, which we had plenty of, we also didn't manage to imbalance in this way.

To summarise, I think it was a game that we didn't deserve to lose. I think a draw would have been something more logical and I think that if there had to be a winner, it should have been us."

-Marcelo Bielsa

The opening fixture in March was another tough challenge. West Ham United were hosting the event at the London Stadium, another ground where the Whites hadn't played before. The men from LS11 had been winless in their last sixteen games in the capital and had lost all of their previous games in London during the current season.

The problem with curses, hoodoos and jinxes is that the longer that the myth perpetuates, the stronger it becomes.

West Ham United 2-0 Leeds United
8th March, 2021

West Ham United
Fabianski, Coufal, Dawson, Diop, Cresswell, Soucek, Rice, Fornals, Lingard (Johnson 87), Benrahma (Bowen 73), Antonio.

Leeds United
Meslier, Ayling, Llorente, Cooper, Dallas, Phillips, Costa (Harrison 45), Roberts (Rodrigo 60), Klich (Alioski 45), Raphinha, Bamford.

Referee: Mike Dean

Kalvin Phillips was back in the team and it wasn't long before our favourite son was in the thick of the action. Helder Costa looked lively and picked out Tyler Roberts, with the Wales international finding the back of the net only for us all to experience the awful sinking feeling that only VAR can give.

Next, Patrick Bamford had the ball in the net. The assist was provided by Raphinha who pulled the ball back from the goal line. This time there was little doubt that the ball had gone out of play.

Too many of United's passes were going astray in midfield and when Liam Cooper sent a wayward ball, Jesse Lingard and Said Benrahma played a neat exchange which caused Luke Ayling to concede a penalty.

LINGARD (21) had his initial effort parried by Illan Meslier, but was able to follow up and open the scoring. Less than seven minutes later, the Hammers doubled their lead.

Aaron Cresswell's free kick was deflected wide of the post by Illan Meslier. The resultant corner found DAWSON (28) at the far post. The big defender rose above Diego Llorente to send a bullet header flying towards the back of the net.

Dawson headed another effort against the post before half time as United floundered. Costa and Klich were withdrawn after the break as both looked like mere shadows of their usual selves.

Gjanni Alioski and Jack Harrison shared the wing back roles and Stuart Dallas moved into midfield. Diego Llorente sent Patrick Bamford through, but the striker curled his shot just past the far post. Shortly afterwards, Raphinha forced Fabianski into a fine save with a spectacular overhead kick.

At the other end, Fornals smashed the ball against the crossbar and United defended a succession of corners. Patrick Bamford then missed another sitter after latching on to a good pass from Raphinha.

Later, he left the ball for Rodrigo but the Spain international was unable to connect with it. By this time it was clear that nothing would be retrieved from this match and the London misery continued.

League Position: 11th

"We had the initial fifteen minutes in the first half, which was the best that we played in the game. We defended well and we attacked well. In the final thirty minutes of the first half, we stopped defending well and it's difficult to attack when you don't defend well.

I think in the second half, we defended and attacked well for the whole of the half. Between the first half and the second half we had sixty minutes of good football. We concede thirty minutes when they attacked, they created danger and managed to score two goals.

I think that if you compare the two periods, we were more dominant in our sixty minute period than they were in their thirty minute period. In the second half, I think we could have drawn and at the start of the first half, we should have scored a goal.

It was difficult to neutralise them in the thirty minutes but if you look at the totality of the game, we deserved something from it."

-Marcelo Bielsa

Chapter Seven
Standout Sequence

Chelsea at Elland Road were next and since the arrival of Thomas Tuchel, the Blues had shown a massive improvement in their form. Impressive wins against Spurs, Liverpool and Everton were recorded, with a newfound confidence since the German coach arrived.

United had gone through the season without losing more than two games consecutively and it seemed that a gargantuan task was in prospect just to maintain this modest record.

Leeds United 0-0 Chelsea
13th March, 2021

Leeds United
Meslier, Ayling, Llorente, Struijk, Alioski, Phillips, Raphinha, Dallas, Roberts, Harrison (Costa 64), Bamford (Rodrigo 35) (Klich 79).

Chelsea
Mendy, Azpilicueta, Christensen, Rudiger, Chilwell, Kante, Jorginho, Pulisic (James 68), Ziyech (Werner 69), Mount (Hudson-Odoi 79), Havertz.

Referee: Kevin Friend

United started this one well, but it was clear that the opposition were going to make life difficult for them and Chelsea dominated the possession throughout the match. Nevertheless, it was the Whites who almost took an early lead.

Patrick Bamford sent Tyler Roberts through and the youngster tapped the ball into the net. However, a disappointing sense of déjà vu abounded as Roberts was denied his moment of glory for the second week running.

It appeared that the miracle of modern science, VAR, judged Bamford to be offside by the narrowest of margins.

Liam Cooper had been unavailable for selection owing to illness and in the first half, Bamford had to leave the field owing to a hip injury.

He was replaced by Rodrigo, who took over the number ten slot from Tyler Roberts. The Wales international had been having a good game but was to lead the line with equal skill.

Both sides had their chances in the first half, but the scoresheet remained blank due to a succession of blocks and the athleticism of two fine goalkeepers.

Pascal Struijk and Diego Llorente were proving a fine partnership in the centre of defence as wave after wave of Chelsea attacks threatened to engulf the Whites.

Ironically, the Blues came closest when Luke Ayling's sliced clearance cannoned off Llorente and over Illan Meslier, only to bounce to safety off the woodwork. The French goalkeeper was also in the thick of the action when he palmed a vicious strike from Kai Havertz over the bar.

At the other end, Edouard Mendy made fine saves from Raphinha and also a tricky deflected effort from Llorente. This was before Rodrigo found himself with a free header from a Raphinha corner, only to head the ball straight at the Chelsea keeper.

United kept running right to the very end and in the final analysis, a well-earned draw was a good and welcome result for them.

League Position: 12th

"Evidently we played against a team that is superior to ours. But in the second half especially, in the first half less, we did what was necessary to play a balanced game, as the chances that both teams had were similar.

It's true that the superiority that they showed in the first half was superior to what we showed in the second half. To be able to play a game like we did today, we had to make an enormous effort. If you take, for example, the last game that Chelsea played before they played us, the first proper chance that they conceded in that game was in the 90th minute.

So for us, to have provoked five or six occasions on goal has its merit."

-Marcelo Bielsa

As I said previously, the problem with legends, myths and curses is that the longer they go on for, the more believable they become. United's well publicised poor record in London was truly shocking.

Since beating Queens Park Rangers in December 2017, The Whites have failed to win a single game in the capital city. Neither the arrival of Marcelo Bielsa, nor the team's elevation to the Premier League had made any difference to this tale of woe.

Whilst the men from LS11 must have been in good heart for their trip to strugglers Fulham, a nagging doubt surely crept in to their collective subconscious. The Cottagers were having problems of their own, though.

Their young manager, Scott Parker, was widely respected for his footballing achievements, if not for his dress sense. The less said about his 'blardigans' (an unlikely combination of a blazer and a cardigan) and tight jackets, the better.

One of the reasons that people liked Parker's team so much is that for a relegation contender, they didn't lose that many games.

In fact, before this clash with United, they had only lost thirteen games which was one less than Bielsa's side. The big problem for the Cottagers was that they didn't win too many games either and their eleven draws was testament to missed opportunities.

Fulham 1-2 Leeds United
19th March, 2021

Fulham
Areola, Aina (Tete 72), Andersen, Tosin, Robinson, Reed (Loftus-Cheek 63), Lemina, Cavaleiro, Zambo, Lookman, Maja (Mitrovic 45).

Leeds United
Meslier, Ayling, Llorente, Struijk, Alioski, Phillips, Raphinha, Dallas, Roberts (Koch 90+3), Harrison, Bamford (Klich 77).

Referee: David Coote

United started in their usual fashion, as they stormed the Fulham defence. Tyler Roberts must really believe that the gods of VAR do not like him. He sent a great cross through to the far post, where Luke Ayling was on hand to head the ball home.

Ayling, who was deputising as captain for Liam Cooper, then loosened his flowing locks for an extravagant celebration for his first Premier League goal. This is the cruellest thing about the delays that are produced by VAR. The spontaneous delight of scoring is now postponed or in this case, cancelled.

Raphinha also had an effort disallowed as he ran on to a Stuart Dallas through ball, to tap the ball into the net. Shortly after these incidents, BAMFORD (29) put United ahead with a well taken effort as he converted a low cross from Jack Harrison.

Fulham fought back gamely, with Josh Maja forcing a fine double save from Illan Meslier before the danger was averted by Luke Ayling. Then, the unthinkable happened and the Cottagers equalised. From the result of a corner, ANDERSEN (38) evaded Luke Ayling's attentions and whacked it in.

In the second half, United took the game by the scruff of the neck and started to dominate. The goal, when it came was straight out of the 'Bielsaball' counter attack textbook.

Kalvin Phillips broke up play on the half way line, releasing Patrick Bamford who in turn sent the speedy RAPHINHA (58) away to whizz past his markers and bury the ball, to put the Whites in front once again.

Shortly afterwards, he had the Fulham defence looking on helplessly as he took the ball right to the byline before cutting it back. Sadly on this occasion, none of his team mates kept up with him and his efforts went in vain.

Patrick Bamford, who had been playing through the pain barrier, left the field on 78 minutes.

He was replaced by Mateusz Klich, who had the luxury of shooting a good chance high and wide. By this time though, the game was heading to its conclusion. United had finally broken the most illogical of spells and had won a game in London.

Hopefully this is the last we hear about this 'curse' which is an unnecessary diversion to the serious business of succeeding in the Premier League.

League Position: 11th

"In the first half up until they scored their equaliser, we were controlling well. After they equalised, there was a segment of confusion from us. The second half was a half with very few fluctuations in the performance. We defended very well after they needed to come back into the game and it was easier for us to attack.

Every game has its motives of why you should dispute them to the maximum. In the last game we were up against a team of quality in Chelsea and today against a team with a necessity for the points, who have been playing well on the back of some good results. For us it was important to win today."

-Marcelo Bielsa

There are few mysteries in modern football, especially in the Premier League where every word and every action is scrutinised by an information-hungry media.

One of the few mysteries was the precise timing and reasons for Chris Wilder's departure from Sheffield United. Wilder had joined the club in May 2016 when the Blades were struggling in League One. It was a dream appointment for him as it was his hometown club.

Within three years, he had led them to the Premier League which was a remarkable achievement in itself. Their maiden Premier League season was the 2019-20 campaign, from which they had finished in an impressive ninth position.

At the start of the current term, they signed players to the value of around £57m and strengthened key positions. This season however, started in a disastrous fashion and carried on in the same vein.

Wilder eventually left by mutual consent on March 13th after protracted negotiations about his payoff. It is even rumoured that he had threatened to resign before Christmas.

If this is true, then 'the boy cried wolf' in order to raise some more money for the January transfer window.

Funds were clearly not forthcoming and having used the 'nuclear option' it is easy to see how an emotional man like Wilder would decide to 'take his ball home'. In any event, the subsequent delay in his departure cannot have done anything to help the club he loved.

The ever-optimistic Paul Heckingbottom took over as caretaker manager and it was very difficult to understand his motivation for doing this. Whatever he achieved at Bramall Lane, it was unlikely to enhance his already tarnished reputation.

At the time of his appointment, Heckingbottom was in charge of the youth team at Bramall Lane. But as Neil Redfearn can testify, it is very difficult to return to a job like that when you have held a senior position at the same club.

Many people understood his reasons for trying his luck at Elland Road, even though it became clear after a short space of time that the job was too big for him. But the caretaker boss at a relegation-doomed club? After his stint with the Whites, he turned up at Hibernian, lasting the best part of a season before being sacked.

This was also a poignant occasion as it marked the first time United had played at Elland Road since the death of Peter Lorimer.

Lorimer still holds the record as United's all time leading scorer (**238 goals**), but even younger fans could relate to him as a result of his regular appearances at the Centenary Pavilion before matches. The Scotsman made his debut against Southampton in 1962 and remains to this day as Leeds United's youngest ever player, playing his first game at just **15 years and 289 days old**.

After the match, Marcelo Bielsa was asked about him and as usual, he expressed a short but fitting tribute which I have included in the Argentine's post-match summary.

Leeds United 2-1 Sheffield United
3rd April, 2021

Leeds United
Meslier, Ayling, Llorente, Cooper, Alioski, Phillips, Raphinha, Dallas (Koch 90+3), Roberts (Klich 81), Harrison, Bamford (Rodrigo 65).

Sheffield United
Ramsdale, Baldock (Ampadu 45), Jagielka, Bogle (Brewster 73), Stevens, Lundstram, Norwood (Burke 65), Fleck, Osborn, McGoldrick, McBurnie (Egan 77).

Referee: Graham Scott

Captain Liam Cooper returned to the team in place of Pascal Struijk and it was impossible not to feel a bit sorry for the impressive Dutch youngster.

But he has time on his side and will have plenty of opportunities in the very near future.

Any result other than a home win would have been a travesty of justice as the Whites started their battering of their opponent's goal as soon as the match began.

Kalvin Phillips was first to test the busy Aaron Ramsdale, who made the first of many saves. Stuart Dallas then tested the Blades keeper before Tyler Roberts found Raphinha with a great pass. The Brazilian waltzed to the byline and sent the ball across to the far post where HARRISON (12) arrived at speed to simply tap it into the net.

Tyler Roberts then put Jack Harrison through with only Ramsdale to beat, but the former Bournemouth man somehow reached the ball to turn it round the post. Shortly afterwards, George Baldock committed a terrible two-footed airborne tackle on Tyler Roberts but as the Sheffield United man landed, he banged his head on the ground.

He left the field to be checked out for concussion and was allowed to return before retiring on the stroke of half time, with blurred vision. In their solicitousness for his welfare, both the referee and the VAR geek forgot to review the incident properly or it would surely have been a red card for Baldock.

Just before half time, Raphinha lost the ball and Gjanni Alioski was unable to dispossess Oliver McBurnie. The big striker then found OSBORN (45+2) at the far post, who had the simple task of nudging the ball home. Before the second period was five minutes old, the Whites regained the lead with a fine move. Luke Ayling found Patrick Bamford, who passed to Tyler Roberts on the right. Roberts teed up Jack Harrison expertly as he raced down the left wing towards the edge of the area.

Harrison sent in a killer cross which was destined for the back of the net and as Raphinha sped towards the danger area, the hapless JAGIELKA (49) could only turn the ball into his own goal. Stuart Dallas then clipped the bar as the Whites continued to batter the Sheffield United defence.

But try as they might, Bielsa's men could not add to their goal tally and it was tempting to think what the score might have been had the Whites been facing ten men for half of the match.

It's also fair to say that the Blades kept the score down by their defensive heroics rather than profligacy on the part of the Whites.

Meetings between these two teams are usually tight affairs and for all of United's dominance, this game was always destined to be another one.

League Position: 11th

"We won by only one goal. When the opponent sees that there is only one goal difference, they arrive a lot in the opponent's goal. We had a sufficient amount of chances to have scored more goals.

Especially many dangerous situations which didn't end in shots that would have increased the options that we would have had to score more goals. But it is very difficult in the Premier League to imagine a more comfortable victory at least for us.

Victories always generate happiness and optimism and when we lose someone, it always generates sadness and memories. It is very difficult for happiness or victory to compensate for the loss of someone, but it's better to have won to say goodbye to such an extraordinary player."

-Marcelo Bielsa

Three big games were to follow; Manchester City (A), Liverpool (H) and Manchester United (H). This cluster of fixtures stood out from the very beginning as being a very tough period for United. In particular, Manchester City looked almost unbeatable, having lost only one game in their last thirty-five in all competitions. They were still involved in both domestic cups, as well as the Champions League.

Manchester City 1-2 Leeds United
10th April, 2021

Manchester City
Ederson, Cancelo, Stones, Ake (Gundogan 58), Mendy (Foden 74), Silva, Fernandinho, Zinchenko, Torres, Jesus, Sterling.

Leeds United
Meslier, Ayling, Llorente, Cooper, Alioski, Phillips, Raphinha (Shackleton 90+6), Dallas, Roberts (Koch 63), Costa, Bamford (Struijk 45+3).

Referee: Andre Marriner

The Whites suffered their lowest share of possession (29%) since Marcelo Bielsa's arrival and seemed to be up against it from the kick off.

England defender John Stones appeared to be playing as an extra forward and seemed to join the City attack at will. Despite having so much of the ball, the Sky Blues seemed to lack their normal killer punch.

United were pressured into a few mistakes with both Illan Meslier and Liam Cooper gifting them with misplaced clearances. Torres headed over the bar from a free kick and Sterling missed a sitter in uncharacteristic style.

Helder Costa then chased after a ball down the left hand side. The winger picked out Patrick Bamford, before the number nine then sent a perfectly weighted pass into the path of DALLAS (42).

The Irishman raced on to it and gleefully smashed the ball into the net via the inside of the post. All of a sudden, United were in dream land. But before they had time to savour the moment, disaster struck.

Liam Cooper flew into a tackle with Gabriel Jesus and although the United captain came out with the ball, he followed through and caught his opponent's knee. Andre Marriner promptly reached for a yellow card which seemed to be a reasonable sanction as we all know that this type of contact is not allowed in the modern game.

The controller of VAR thought differently and Marriner was called back to watch the replay of the incident on the monitor. The slow motion sequence that he witnessed made the offence look worse and shortly afterwards, Mariner produced a red card.

United were now tasked with holding a lead for forty-five minutes against one of the best sides on the planet. This task would be difficult enough with a full side, but with ten men it seemed almost impossible.

The unfortunate Patrick Bamford was withdrawn to make way for Pascal Struijk and later ,Robin Koch replaced Tyler Roberts to give the Whites a firmer defensive line.

As was expected, City took up residence in the United half, but the Whites put on an epic defensive effort and repelled everything that was thrown at them. Kalvin Phillips and Illan Meslier stood out in a defence who kept Guardiola's side at bay.

Inevitably, the home side took advantage of the situation and a slick move was completed by TORRES (76) who levelled the game. The Whites now had to try to hold out for a draw.

This possibility was also against all the odds because like all good teams, Manchester City had a nasty habit of sneaking in late winners with little time left on the clock.

The Whites finally made a break as Raphinha raced forward and found himself with only Ederson to beat. Sadly, the City keeper made a world class save and denied his fellow Brazilian.

Somehow, justice was done and a nice piece of United's history was written in the Etihad Stadium.

As the minutes stole by, Gjanni Alioski sent a defence splitting through ball to DALLAS (90+1). Cookstown's finest ran on to it and dispatched the ball into the net, through Ederson's open legs.

Even in the modern era, even in the Premier League, miracles do happen. United triumphed against all the odds and knocked City off their lofty perch despite being reduced to ten men with half of the match left.

A result that will be remembered for many years.

League Position: 10th

"I think the dominance of the game corresponded to City. The chances that went in were also in their favour and with these two arguments, if City had won, it would have been fair.

But we think that the result the team obtained was deserved because of the character, the personality, the effort, the fortitude from a mental point of view and a physical point of view.

It's a little bit strange to say that it would have been fair for City to win but we deserved to win and I would like to explain that. The reason why I believe that we deserved to win was because of the belief of the players that they could do it.

That Leeds beat Manchester City doesn't mean I imposed myself over their manager. That Guardiola is the manager of the team that Leeds beat today, I don't consider anything on my part. What I do give great value to is the players who managed to win such a difficult game especially given the circumstances of being one man down."

-Marcelo Bielsa

Over the same weekend, the news broke that six English clubs had signed an agreement to join the 'European Super League' competition.

The clubs in question were Arsenal, Chelsea, Liverpool, Manchester City, Manchester United and Tottenham Hotspur. Across the continent, they were joined by Atletico Madrid, Barcelona, Real Madrid, AC Milan, Inter Milan and Juventus.

The idea was that in addition to the new competition, they would continue to participate in current competitions. To the bemused onlooker, the formulation of this new league's membership seemed to be based on a combination of historic performance in the Champions League, how much debt they were in and how greedy they were.

The worst feature of the proposed 'league' was that it was a closed shop with no promotion in or relegation out. From the beginning, the owners of these clubs had no idea of the negative backlash that they would receive from supporters of all clubs, including their own.

A full scale demonstration took place outside Elland Road on the night of the Liverpool game, with supporters from several clubs involved. United ran out to warm up in tops with messages that read: *"UEFA Champions League - Earn It"* (Front) *"Football Is For The Fans"* (Back)

A set of these t-shirts was left in the away changing room, but Liverpool did not take up the offer! The chief suspect in 'Shirtgate' was the irrepressible Victor Orta, who continually waved a shirt about throughout the match.

It was impossible not to feel sorry for Jurgen Klopp though, as he was interviewed about the situation before the match. He had made his opposition to such a plan clear previously, but was now in the invidious position of being asked to publicly disagree with his employers.

This season proved to be quite a comedown for the Reds who had set a new club record of six home defeats in a row between January and March. Despite leading the pack going into 2021, the reigning champions suddenly found themselves twenty-two points behind Manchester City.

Leeds United 1-1 Liverpool
19th April, 2021

Leeds United
Meslier, Ayling, Llorente, Struijk, Alioski (Klich 79), Phillips, Costa (Poveda 67), Dallas, Roberts (Hernandez 86), Harrison, Bamford.

Liverpool
Alisson, Alexander-Arnold, Fabinho, Kabak, Robertson, Thiago, Wijnaldum, Milner, Jota (Oxlade-Chamberlain), Firmino, Mane (Salah 71).

Referee: Anthony Taylor

Liverpool started well with both Firmino and Fabinho coming close. Kalvin Phillips was as alert as ever to a counter attack opportunity and sent Patrick Bamford away.

Unfortunately, the striker's first touch was heavy and Alisson was able to smother the shot.

At the other end, Trent Alexander-Arnold rounded Jack Harrison and then Illan Meslier, before leaving the advancing MANE (31) with the simple task of slotting the ball home.

United were struggling with Liverpool's press and seemed to be missing the pace of Raphinha. Creativity in other parts of the field was lacking and Tyler Roberts was having a very quiet game.

Ian Poveda replaced Helder Costa for the second half, but it was Jack Harrison who had the first opportunity for United. He played a smart exchange with Tyler Roberts, before seeing his shot beaten away by Alisson at the near post.

Luke Ayling then found Patrick Bamford in the Liverpool penalty area, but the striker lofted the ball on to Alisson's crossbar. As time wore on, the Whites kept fighting but it was starting to look like a narrow defeat, but this side just don't know when they are beaten.

A late corner was awarded to the Whites. Jack Harrison whipped it across with great pace and LLORENTE (87) rose above the Liverpool defence to head it home. After such an unlucky start with injuries, his performances have been very poised and classy.

The goal was the icing on the cake and I feel that it will stay in his memory for an awfully long time. The first game of the season may have been thrilling, but United are showing a new solidity in defence. After a mediocre first half, the Whites dominated the second period and would have won if they had taken their chances.

League Position: 10th

"I think the game was beautiful. In the first half, it was more even and in the second half we managed to dominate proceedings.

We created opportunities and we played in the opponent's half. We recovered many balls that permitted us or allowed us to attack. But it's also true that while we were managing proceedings, they maintained their threat.

Of course it (a European Super League) damages football. This should not surprise any of us. The stronger teams think they have the most influence in generating revenue in football and if you take into account this logic, when the rest of the teams are no longer necessary for them, they take privilege in their own interests and they forget about the rest."

-Marcelo Bielsa

Thankfully, before twenty-four hours had elapsed, the 'Super League' idea was dead in the water and eventually all of the participants in England took part in an embarrassing climb down.

The remaining worry was that the scheme would reappear at some stage in the future under some other guise, but having shown their hand to the public, the plotters would find it more difficult to get away with something this outrageous again.

Football has a habit of throwing up coincidences and Manchester United, arguably the biggest club of the 'greedy six' were the next visitors to Elland Road. Earlier in the season, they had subjected the Whites to their heaviest defeat of the campaign so far, but they were facing a far tighter unit this time.

Leeds United 0-0 Manchester United
25th April, 2021

Leeds United
Meslier, Ayling, Llorente, Struijk, Alioski, Phillips,
Costa (Klich 72), Dallas, Roberts (Koch 77),
Harrison (Poveda 78), Bamford.

Manchester United
Henderson, Wan-Bissaka, Lindelof, Maguire, Shaw,
McTominay, Fred, James (Pogba 76), Fernandes,
Rashford (Cavani 86), Greenwood.

Referee: Craig Pawson

Raphinha was unable to start again after his clash
with Fernandinho of Manchester City. He was
replaced once more by Helder Costa, before the
former Wolves man was clattered himself, half way
through the second period.

There was a feeling that the Manchester United
players were fairly confident of taking three points
again if not winning by the same margin. As the
game wore on, it became clear that our United were
not going to go along with the plan.

The Whites have added the ability to fight a
rearguard action to their other list of skills. Even so,
they had their moments. Jack Harrison sent in a fine
cross towards Costa, but the ball was deflected to
safety courtesy of Luke Shaw's outstretched arm.

However, Mike Dean on VAR did not see it as a deliberate hand ball.

Shortly afterwards, Stuart Dallas shot straight at Dean Henderson in the Manchester United goal and then failed to find Jack Harrison with a pass after Lindelof had gifted it to Patrick Bamford.

Both Luke Ayling and Tyler Roberts both received yellow cards as the Red Devils continued to press, before Marcus Rashford drew a fine save from Illan Meslier to end a mediocre first half.

Before leaving the field, Helder Costa was in the thick of things at both ends of the pitch. He was beaten by Aaron Wan-Bissaka, who laid the ball on for Fernandes, who squandered his chance. Helder Costa's own deflected shot only just cleared the crossbar, as the game swung from end-to-end.

The game became bad tempered and scrappy as the temperatures rose and Manchester United's frustrations increased. The talented, but unpredictable Paul Pogba was then introduced to the game, but the Whites countered his threat by bringing on Robin Koch.

Gjanni Alioski made a huge block on a Mason Greenwood shot as the clock ran down. This game was not a classic, but United could mark it down as a significant improvement on their previous encounter with their biggest rivals.

League Position: 9th

"It was a very demanding game for us. For the game not to become unbalanced, the team made a massive effort. This effort allowed the game not to become unbalanced for us. The game for them came more naturally for them.

I insist that I value a lot of everything that we did so that the game would not become unbalanced. What was touching or moving today was the effort that the team made. A game like today, if we did not bring big energy, we wouldn't be able to balance it.

The players have constructed a solid group. Throughout this time they have made errors and learned how to correct them. And in the same way, they have learned how to avoid the errors that are avoidable. I have the feeling that there has been a growth in the maturity in their experience to manage these games."

-Marcelo Bielsa

Chapter Eight
Closing Clashes

A trip to the South Coast to face Brighton & Hove Albion was next for the Whites. This seemed a fairly mundane prospect after the teams that United had faced recently.

The Seagulls were still fighting to ensure their safety and had drawn with Everton and Chelsea, before losing to the doomed Sheffield United. In many ways, this was the story of their season, consistency having been their biggest problem.

Trips to their Amex Stadium in the recent past were never much fun for United Supporters. The games were invariably scheduled for midweek kick offs, which caused maximum inconvenience for many Whites fans.

In theory, a trip their state-of-the-art stadium with its own dedicated train station at Falmer should have been a pleasure. Instead, it ended up being like a trip to Millwall.

The Albion fans were generally much better behaved than their counterparts in South London. Their worst actions seemed to be singing a couple of tuneless verses of 'Sussex by the Sea' after consuming a couple of halves of Harvey's Bitter.

Despite this, the club officials and police corralled fans into pens after the match until every single home fan had caught their train into town.

Of course, nobody would have this problem today and I began to think that maybe the place was not that bad after all!

Brighton & Hove Albion 2-0 Leeds United
1st May, 2021

Brighton & Hove Albion
Sanchez, Dunk, Webster, White, Veltman, Gross, Bissouma (Mac Allister 90+2), Burn, Trossard (Jahanbakhsh 80), Maupay, Welbeck (Moder 90).

Leeds United
Meslier, Ayling, Llorente (Hernandez 79), Struijk, Alioski, (Poveda 45), Koch, Dallas, Klich, Roberts, Harrison, Bamford (Rodrigo 59).

Referee: Chris Kavanagh

The game against the Seagulls at Elland Road back in January was one of United's worst performances of the season. This showing was even poorer.

The Whites seemed to be jaded and looked like a collection of players who were dreaming of their summer holidays. It was just not the sort of performance that was expected from a team coached by Marcelo Bielsa.

The problem of replacing an injured Kalvin Phillips seemed no nearer to being solved. Robin Koch did his best and broke up several Brighton attacks, but linking attack and defence did not happen for him for most of the game. Maybe the German international will grow into the role.

Raphinha and his recent deputy, Helder Costa, were also missed and although Stuart Dallas toiled away in his original position of right wing, he made very little impression.

On the left side of the pitch, Jack Harrison was having an unusually quiet game as well. When Gjanni Alioski stumbled in the penalty area and brought Danny Welbeck down in a crab-like scrambling motion, the referee pointed unhesitatingly to the spot.

GROSS (14) converted the kick and although Illan Meslier got a hand to the ball, the shot was just too powerful for him.

Shortly afterwards, Trossard had a shot which was well held by Meslier and as the game staggered to the half way mark, there was little positivity from either side.

At least Brighton were getting a few shots away, whereas the United attacks were being stifled before they had a chance to get going. Alioski was subbed at half time and Ian Poveda took the wide role over from Stuart Dallas, but it made little difference.

The game could have easily been over on the hour, had the Seagulls been able to convert one of their many chances. Pascal Struijk then failed to clear his lines. WELBECK (79) latched on to the ball, turned well and struck the ball firmly past Illan Meslier.

United had no more to offer and did not even deserve a point from this encounter.

League Position: 11th

"Fundamentally, today's performance was due to a certain sector on the pitch where we couldn't prevent their three centre backs from playing the ball out cleanly, nor could we overcome them.

Our game in attack was very weak. I always think that when we don't attack well or defend well it's a collective problem. The passing from front to back wasn't clean, nor could we win the ball back in their half so that we could make them a little more disorganised because they were very organised.

Their three centre backs protected the wide areas. They protected the backs of their two defensive midfielders and they always managed to bring the ball out when the goalkeeper didn't go long."

-Marcelo Bielsa

For most football fans who follow teams in the top two tiers, the decline of the three o'clock Saturday games is something that they greatly miss.

In more normal times when supporters are able to watch their favourites live, the away matches are often a great adventure and the trip, the drinks and the game itself is often a memorable experience.

Home matches however, are different. Most fans follow a comfortable and sometimes superstitious ritual. Few fans want to make any changes. They use the same pubs, set off at the same time and attend the match with the same people.

Long before I was interested in pursuing girls or consuming beer, I followed a sacred and unchangeable ritual myself. The routine actually started about twelve thirty on Friday at school. Just before we had our lunchtime break, our form master, Father O'Callaghan would post a small slip on the class notice board.

As soon as the bell was rung, I would rush to the front to make sure that I had been selected for the class football team to play the following day. On Saturday morning, I would shovel some breakfast cereal into my mouth, check the contents of my duffel bag, before running to the bottom of Gathorne Street to catch the bus into town.

Although 'St Micks' was in the Woodhouse/Hyde Park area of Leeds, the playing fields were out at Cookridge and so another bus was taken to this destination. The game duly took place and all of the scruffy urchins, including myself, were forced to have a communal bath.

I can still smell the carbolic soap and see the mud and grass from eleven filthy boys floating on the surface of the lukewarm water. There was very little horseplay as most of us just wanted to get out and be warm and dry again.

The bus was then caught back into Leeds, where I made my way to Youngman's Fish bar. It was situated on Queen Victoria Street, not far from the County Arcade. This institution opened in 1885 before finally closing in 1989. Upstairs there was a sit down restaurant where the more well-heeled could dine, but on the ground floor there was a great hall which was surrounded by shelves on the wall.

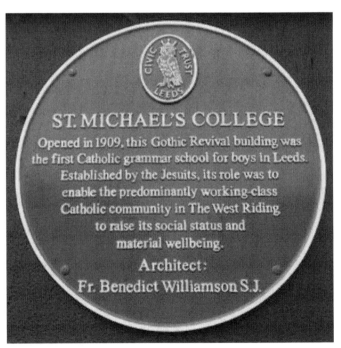

The plaque outside my alma mater 'St. Mick's' in Leeds.

This meant that even in poor weather, you could eat your fish and chips from the paper at your leisure. It was in this establishment that I met my brother and other pals, who went to different schools.

The 52 bus was then taken from the Corn Exchange to Elland Road, where we headed for the Kop. If we managed to arrive early enough, a place could be found at the front where you could lean on the whitewashed wall.

To alleviate the boredom while we waited for the kick off, we would stick a penny to the ground with chewing gum and watch old boys struggling as they tried to pick it up.

After the match, we would wait behind until all the crowd had dispersed. We would then climb up into the West Stand. In those days, very few adults collected football programmes. After the game, the well-heeled patrons of the West Stand would just discard the programmes, usually dropping them on the floor.

I could usually harvest about thirty or so and as I was the only collector among us, my brother and my pals would give me the ones that they found. 'Soccer Star' was a weekly football magazine that was published between 1952 and 1970. 'Swaps' could be advertised free of charge and so I ran a weekly ad that offered two United programmes in exchange for any other League team's programme.

All the other children had to do was supply me with a stamped addressed envelope, along with the programme that they sent me and I would send them two of my surplus United programmes.

When we left or were thrown out of the ground, we would walk into town to await the arrival of Saturday's sports papers. In those days, there were two sports papers: The Yorkshire Evening News (green) and the Yorkshire Evening Post (buff).

My brother and I would buy one of each before swapping them later in the evening. One or the other would also be commandeered by my Dad when he returned home from work.

He showed little interest in most sports, but needed to check his football pools. It was a never-ending source of amazement to him that my brother and I were unable to help him to become rich.

Our assistance had been sought a couple of times before he realised that we were of no use whatsoever as tipsters.
"With what all you fellers know about football and you can't even pick out eight bloody draws....."

After the Brighton game, the 'glass half empty brigade' were out in force. According to them, the massive efforts expended in putting together an unbeaten run in the last six games had finally taken its toll on the Whites.

What they were not taking into consideration was the resilience that United had shown throughout the season and their ability to bounce back after a poor performance. Nevertheless, Spurs were formidable opposition under any circumstances.

Leeds United 3-1 Tottenham Hotspur
8th May, 2021

Leeds United
Meslier, Ayling, Llorente, Struijk, Alioski, Koch, Dallas, Roberts (Raphinha 58), Klich (Phillips 90), Harrison, Bamford (Rodrigo 79).

Tottenham Hotspur
Lloris, Aurier, Alderweireld, Dier, Reguilon, Lo Celso (Ndombele 80), Hojbjerg, Bale (Moura 67), Alli (Lamela 67), Son, Kane.

Referee: Michael Oliver

Although Raphinha and Kalvin Phillips were available, they did not start. Robin Koch continued in the holding midfield role and Stuart Dallas played wide once again. Gjanni Alioski, who had been withdrawn at half time against the Seagulls, was restored to an unchanged United Side.

The North Macedonian turned out to be one of the stars of this particular show. United may have plumbed the depths against Brighton, but against the men from North London, they reached the dizziest heights and looked a totally different team.

Early in the half, Alioski played the ball to Dallas on the right. The Irishman returned the compliment, before Jack Harrison was sent charging down the left. The Manchester City loanee then placed one of his killer crosses into the box.

Sergio Reguilon could only lunge at the ball as he saw it heading towards goal Lloris was at hand to claw the ball away, but only into the path of DALLAS (13), who gleefully smashed the ball inside the roof of the net. It was a great move and a classic example of Bielsaball.

A period of pressure came from Spurs and this culminated in an equaliser. Dele Alli celebrated his return to the side by sending SON (25) through to rifle a fine shot past Illan Meslier.

Not long after, Alli then found Harry Kane, who raced into the United penalty area and netted the ball. Thankfully after a VAR check, offside was declared by the finest of margins, leaving the Whites to breathe again.

United set up another fine move and again, Gjanni Alioski was in the thick of it. Stuart Dallas won the ball in the Spurs half and found Tyler Roberts. The Wales international then passed to Harrison, who instinctively released Alioski on the overlap. The North Macedonian then performed a perfect cutback to the arriving BAMFORD (42), who scored a striker's goal straight out of the textbook.

During the initial period of the second half, Spurs were doing their best to fight back. The redoubtable Harry Kane had the ball in the net and once again offside was given, although there was little doubt about it this time. Son was also in a good position during this spell, but thankfully he shot wide.

As the visitors chased an equaliser, United took full advantage of the gaps that were beginning to appear. Mateusz Klich saw a good effort denied by Hugo Lloris. At the other end, Illan Meslier earned his keep with a fine save from Serge Aurier before Harry Kane clipped the crossbar with a free kick.

But Spurs were beginning to tire and United introduced the fresh legs of Raphinha and Rodrigo. Alioski then won the ball in his own half and sent the ball to Klich, who found Robin Koch in the middle of the park.

Koch sent a Phillips-like raking ball to Raphinha who galloped away, before squaring it to the grateful RODRIGO (84) and United's record signing smashed it into the bottom left corner.

There was no longer any doubt about the result of the game. Spurs were a spent force and had nothing more to offer.

Robin Koch had played the holding midfield role to perfection and it seemed that an answer to the conundrum about cover for Kalvin Phillips had finally been found.

Phillips himself was not required in this game, but did come on in the 90th minute with a big smile on his face, to join his colleagues in celebration of a great result.

League Position: 10th

"Considering the fortitude of the opponent and the way in which we attacked and defended and the possibilities to play pretty much on even terms, it's one of the best performances of the season.

The performance in the last game was an unexpected one for us. I think the level of production did not correspond to the level of the players that we had on the field. I thought it was considered to maintain the same eleven players.

We could have scored more goals but we could also have conceded some more as well. I think that the difference of two goals is adequate and fair. To have won by more goals would not have corresponded even if it was possible. To have won by only one goal, I don't think that this would have been fair either but they could have closed the distance too."

-Marcelo Bielsa

I have always felt that the grimness of the former East Lancashire mill towns is more than compensated by the warmth and friendliness of their people. Of the towns, Burnley is my favourite.

This is because Turf Moor was my first destination for an away match in December 1959, during the relegation season. At the time, United were the only Yorkshire team in the old First Division and so Burnley were our nearest neighbours.

When I had asked my Dad if I could go, he had immediately said yes. This was due to my perfect timing, as I had asked his permission when he had returned bathed in the afterglow that only a couple of beers can produce. Nevertheless, following school the next afternoon I went straight down to Wallace Arnold's old offices below the Corn Exchange and bought my coach ticket.

There were a couple of threats to my proposed trip. Firstly, as my elder brother was not around, I was going on my own and even more worryingly it was only five days before Christmas and my school reports were due any day.

The Saturday was a cold and drizzly day and it rained all afternoon, but I enjoyed every minute of it. Jack Overfield scored the only goal of the game and gave United hopes of survival. I even enjoyed the coach trip back and seeing all the Christmas lights in Todmorden and Halifax, as I cleaned the condensation off the coach window with my sleeve.

Sadly United only won two more away games that season, but I was well and truly hooked. Although the likes of Rotherham and Scunthorpe would be my among my trips the following year.

155

Fast forward to 2021 and Sean Dyche went into this game as the current longest serving Premier League Manager at seven years, but he also managed Burnley in the Championship for an additional twenty-four months.

He is widely respected in the game for his ability to run a team on a fairly limited wage bill. Although it's not that long ago that United were in such a poor position financially that he was able to pop over the Pennines and relieve them of the services of Chris Wood and Charlie Taylor.

Burnley 0-4 Leeds United
15th May, 2021

Burnley
Peacock-Farrell, Lowton, Tarkowski, Mee, Taylor, Brownhill, Westwood, Cork, McNeil (Gudmundsson 70), Vydra (Rodriguez 65), Wood (Barnes 65).

Leeds United
Meslier, Ayling, Llorente, Struijk, Dallas, Phillips, Alioski, Raphinha (Poveda 81), Klich (Roberts 76), Harrison, Bamford (Rodrigo 58).

Referee: Graham Scott

Bailey Peacock-Farrell started for Burnley, making only his fourth appearance of the season for the Clarets, having been kept out of the team by England international, Nick Pope.

Peacock-Farrell played between the sticks for United for the first half of Marcelo Bielsa's debut season at Elland Road. But the young Northern Ireland international lost his place when the Whites signed Kiko Casilla and moved to Burnley before the 2019-20 season.

United were starting with a strong line up but this was expected to be a dour game, even though Burnley were now safe from the threat of relegation. That is exactly how the game began. Burnley started well in the uncompromising style that we have come to know if not exactly love.

Struijk came closest with an effort which just found its way past the wrong side of the post, as the game settled into a morass of midfield mediocrity. It was KLICH (44) that broke the spell with a fine individual effort.

He ran from the halfway line and as the Clarets defence backed away from him, he let fly with a scorching effort which was reminiscent of some of the fine goals he scored in the last couple of seasons. He has also risen from his dip in form in the last couple of weeks and it was good to see him looking happy and confident.

In the second half, United nearly came a cropper when Matej Vydra found himself with only Illan Meslier to beat. Thankfully, the Frenchman thwarted his effort with a fine save as he stuck one of his long legs out and sent the ball to safety.

Just before the hour mark, Patrick Bamford was replaced by Rodrigo. Bamford was having an uncharacteristically torrid time of it and nothing was going well for him. In contrast, Rodrigo looked sharp and almost latched on to a cross from Jack Harrison. From the resultant corner, the ball came to Gjanni Alioski who sent a wayward shot into the penalty area.

Although HARRISON (59) had his back to goal, he managed to back heel it past the bemused Peacock-Farrell and into the net. Harrison then sent a sublime through ball which split the Burnley central defenders. RODRIGO (77) took it in his stride, before dinking it in for number three.

As Burnley reeled, Kalvin Phillips found Jack Harrison as he raced down the left flank. The Manchester City loanee sent another precise ball into the path of RODRIGO (79), who danced around Peacock-Farrell to make it his third goal in two matches.

Near the end, there was a bizarre incident where Gjanni Alioski was involved in a minor scuffle with Dwight McNeil. When Alioski got to his feet, he pulled a childish face at the Burnley man who was later substituted.

Although the referee called both managers together, little was said except that an 'incident' had been reported by a Burnley player. It really is time that these guys grew up.

Nothing should be allowed to detract from United's stunning performance. Sean Dyche, of course, gave Bielsa's side no credit whatsoever. Despite his obvious attributes as a coach and manager, it seems impossible for him to be gracious and acknowledge when his team has been well beaten.

League Position: 10th

"Particularly in the first half we gave a great defensive performance. Even though we conceded a few more chances in the second half which we didn't in the first I think that the fact was that they attacked with more insistence.

The resolution of the central part of the back three was very important and also the contribution of our goalkeeper. Mateusz Klich played a very good game against Tottenham and he kept the same level in the game today. He's at a similar level to his best level within this team. It gives me great happiness that he is playing as he is capable of playing."

-Marcelo Bielsa

United's final away game of the season took place at St. Mary's. For the first half of their campaign, Southampton hovered around the European spots. But since the turn of the year, they picked up seventeen points from twenty games before their clash with United. As a result, the Saints found themselves in sixteenth position, whereas the Whites were looking to seal a top half finish.

Southampton 0-2 Leeds United
18th May, 2021

Southampton
McCarthy, Walker-Peters, Stephens, Vestergaard, Salisu, Walcott (Diallo 78), Ward-Prowse, Armstrong, Djenepo, Adams (Ings 45), Tella (Redmond 70).

Leeds United
Casilla, Ayling, Llorente (Berardi 45), Cooper, Dallas, Phillips (Struijk 45), Alioski, Raphinha, Rodrigo (Roberts 78), Harrison, Bamford.

Referee: Peter Bankes

Kiko Casilla was recalled to the side to give Illan Meslier a rest after a successful season. Whether the French youngster actually wanted to have a rest, we shall never know.

Mateusz Klich and Robin Koch were also given an early holiday. The former definitely needed a rest after his many appearances, whereas Robin Koch had taken a slight knock against Burnley. It was hoped that both players would be fit for selection for their countries in the forthcoming European Championship fixtures.

The game started in a similar fashion to the Burnley match in that the home side dominated the possession and the proceedings in general.

Like Burnley, the Saints did not convert this endeavour into any meaningful chances. Those that were on target were dealt with by Kiko Casilla, starting with a strong header from Che Adams which the Spanish keeper tipped over the bar.

It was Adams again who tested Casilla, who saved the ball in the bottom corner. In fact, the Spaniard was having a successful afternoon apart from a couple of attempts to rescue crosses where he didn't end up with the ball.

United for their part did little to trouble Alex McCarthy in the first forty-five minutes. In the second half, Diego Llorente and Kalvin Phillips were replaced by Pascal Struijk and the ever-reliable Gaetano Berardi.

'The Warrior' was moving on at the end of the season and had been a very loyal player who always gave everything to the club. Marcelo Bielsa is not in the sentimentality business and so, as expected Berardi had a fine second half.

Patrick Bamford had a heavy collision with Mohammed Salisu and was on the floor for some time before picking himself up. Shortly afterwards, Bamford tried to get around Alex McCarthy.

The Southampton keeper impeded his progress and pushed Bamford wide, meaning he could not get a meaningful shot or cross away.

Bamford was penalised for his honesty and told the referee this in no uncertain terms. Had he thrown himself to the floor a penalty would have been given. Peter Bankes does not bear the sole responsibility for this, because the VAR operative must have picked this up also.

However, justice was done as BAMFORD (73) picked up on a through ball from Rodrigo and slotted the ball between McCarthy's legs from an angle just as tight as the one in the penalty incident.

For the final period, the game swung from end to end. But it was United who landed the killer punch, which started from a Saints free kick.

Jack Stephens had a golden opportunity to equalise for the home side, but could only head straight at Casilla. Instead of holding on to the ball and killing a few more seconds, the Spaniard immediately started a breakaway for United after finding Raphinha on the right hand side.

The winger then released the ball at the precise moment to play in Tyler Roberts. Although he had been dispossessed in the penalty area just before he was about to shoot, the ball fell to Bamford who hit a ferocious effort towards goal.

McCarthy could only parry the ball to a grateful ROBERTS (90+5). The youngster made no mistake this time and gleefully passed it into the net for his first Premier League goal.

Bielsa made no secret of his delight, because Roberts has been extremely unlucky in front of goal this season, often through no fault of his own.

League Position: 10th

"It was not my influence, it was the profile of individual players in the second half that changed the game. I was happy that Tyler Roberts scored because he had played many games and he hadn't managed to do it.

Also, just how we unlevelled the game in the second half, Southampton could have done the same in the first half. The fact that Kiko played today and will play Sunday is a decision that I decided to make concrete. Berardi is in an excellent state of form. Him coming on was very useful, he didn't commit errors and he added a lot."

-Marcelo Bielsa

After a season that flew by, the final game had finally arrived. Eight thousand lucky fans had been allowed to buy tickets for the match and one thing that was beyond dispute was that those supporters would make more noise than any rivals who had been admitted to their grounds.

It was also an occasion tinged with sadness as it was time to say goodbye to two stalwarts of the club; Pablo Hernandez and Gaetano Berardi. They had served Leeds United in different ways.

Hernandez will be remembered for his silky skills and goals, particularly the one against Swansea in July 2020 which all but sealed United's promotion to the Premier League. Berardi arrived in LS11 as a hard working, but indisciplined journeyman who kicked first and asked questions afterwards.

Gradually he cleaned up his act without losing the grit and determination that made him a fans favourite from the beginning. Marcelo Bielsa completed Berardi's education by giving him extra skills, most notably the ability to play in the centre of defence. When he sustained a serious injury against Derby County in the penultimate game of last season, Andrea Radrizzani stood by him and extended the defender's contract by one year.

Leeds United 3-1 West Bromwich Albion
23rd May, 2021

Leeds United
Casilla, Berardi (Struijk 69), Ayling, Cooper, Raphinha, Dallas, Phillips, Alioski, Hernandez (Roberts 70), Harrison, Rodrigo (Bamford 45).

West Bromwich Albion
Johnstone, Furlong, Ajayi, Bartley, O'Shea (Robson-Kanu 60), Townsend, Gallagher, Yokuslu, Maitland-Niles (Grant 83), Phillips, Robinson (Diangana 61).

Referee: David Coote

As expected, Gaetano Berardi and Pablo Hernandez started the game, with both of them well worth their place in the side. Kiko Casilla continued in goal and Rodrigo started in the role of lone striker.

The game started with some good possession by the visitors and they were awarded a free kick after only twenty seconds. Liam Cooper also received a booking for his reckless challenge on Darnell Furlong. Former United favourite, Kyle Bartley headed wide from the resultant set piece before the Whites started to gain control of the match.

Just after a quarter of an hour, Hernandez sent Jack Harrison away with a sublime pass. The Manchester City loanee had the ball in the net but was judged to be offside. But it was not long before United took the initiative. Raphinha delivered a perfect corner and RODRIGO (17) headed home at the far post.

For the first time, Rodrigo was able to celebrate with the fans and it was a very welcome sight. Kalvin Phillips doesn't score many goals, but he seems to score them on momentous occasions. The centenary match last season against Birmingham City comes to mind as a good example.

Hernandez won a free kick for the Whites and it would have been no surprise if he had taken the kick himself. However, PHILLIPS (42) stepped up and hit the ball towards goal.

Without taking anything away from Phillips, Sam Johnstone in the Baggies goal should have made a better job of it as the ball took a wicked bounce before landing in the net.

Rodrigo was withdrawn at half time and replaced by Patrick Bamford. The Spaniard had scored four goals in the last three games and was beginning to look like the player that we all hoped he would be.

Pablo Hernandez's teammates tried desperately to tee him up for one of his trade mark goals. But try as he might, the little magician could not find the net, mostly thanks to the efforts of Sam Johnstone.

Hernandez and Berardi were both substituted with just over twenty minutes to go and received the ovation that they deserved. Unashamed tears were shed by both players, most of the crowd and no doubt many television viewers all over the world.

When Okay Yokuslu blatantly handled a Harrison cross, BAMFORD (79) stepped up and dispatched the penalty to start the party.

But as the game was about to reach injury time, the best player on the pitch, Kalvin Phillips, then carried out an unscripted action. The 'Yorkshire Pirlo' allowed a pass from Cooper to run under his feet. As a result, ROBSON-KANU (90) was able to run in and cooly slot the ball home.

Worse was to come, just a couple of minutes later. Phillips, clearly frustrated by his error, went flying into a tackle and ended up getting booked. He also landed heavily on his shoulder and left the field in pain, meaning he was unable to take part in the lap of appreciation. Nearly a perfect day, but not quite.

"It's difficult to offer a conclusion, because on one side I am very satisfied with what the team achieved but on the other side, I feel like we could have added a few more points. If we divided the competition in two, in the second part of the season we received fifteen percent less of the goals than we did in the first part. Had we had that security defensively in the whole campaign, we could have added those points I would have liked.

The performance of Pablo today indicates that he deserved more minutes than I gave him this year. Berardi, after such a long time without playing, showed he can still be current but the most important thing is that the public, teammates and the staff showed recognition to those two players.

You can play very well and be a great player but to be a great professional and to become a reference in a place where you have played, what's missing is to be a good human. I always thought that there are loads of great players but great professionals who stamp their imprint on a club are those who apart from playing well are good people."

-Marcelo Bielsa

The victory against West Bromwich Albion cemented a ninth place finish for United, confirmed in the final league table below.

Position	Team	Played	Points	
1 (C)	Manchester City	38	86	^
2	Manchester United	38	74	^
3	Liverpool	38	69	^
4	Chelsea	38	67	^
5	Leicester City	38	66	~
6	West Ham United	38	65	~
7	Tottenham Hotspur	38	62	*
8	Arsenal	38	61	
9	Leeds United	38	59	
10	Everton	38	59	
11	Aston Villa	38	55	
12	Newcastle United	38	45	
13	Wolverhampton Wanderers	38	45	
14	Crystal Palace	38	44	
15	Southampton	38	43	
16	Brighton & Hove Albion	38	41	
17	Burnley	38	39	
18 (R)	Fulham	38	28	
19 (R)	West Bromwich Albion	38	26	
20 (R)	Sheffield United	38	23	

^	Champions League Group Stage Qualification
~	Europa League Group Stage Qualification
*	Europa Conference League Play-Off Qualification

As well as accumulating the highest points tally for a side promoted to the Premier League since 2001, there were new records set at both ends of the pitch.

Chapter Nine
Ending Endorsements

After the goalless draw with Manchester United in April 2021, Illan Meslier became the youngest goalkeeper in Premier League history to reach ten clean sheets in a season. Also, once the campaign had concluded, only four goalkeepers recorded more clean sheets than the young Frenchman.

At the other end, the Whites scored sixty-two goals, which is a new record for a promoted team across a thirty-eight game Premier League season. The standout contributor was undoubtedly Patrick Bamford, who racked up seven assists alongside his seventeen goals.

Listed below is a summary for all the Leeds United players involved in an extraordinary first season back in the top flight.

Stuart Dallas   38 Appearances (38 Starts)
Player of the Year in a season when there were several contenders. 'The Cookstown Cafu' doesn't just play in different positions, he excels in them.

Luke Ayling   38 Appearances (38 Starts)
Took to the Premier League like a duck to water. A reliable vice captain and never afraid to get forward.

Patrick Bamford   38 Appearances (37 Starts)
Confounded his critics with seventeen Premier
League goals. There is so much more to his game,
with his assists and work in attack and defence.

Illan Meslier   35 Appearances (35 Starts)
Worthy winner of the Young Player of the Year
award, with maturity far beyond his years.

Jack Harrison   36 Appearances (34 Starts)
Another player whose star is definitely on the rise.
He has improved considerably on his impressive
performance last season.

Gjanni Alioski   36 Appearances (29 Starts)
Although he is prone to the odd lapse, he always
gives everything and surprises with his energetic
and skilful displays. A great asset to any side.

Mateusz Klich   35 Appearances (28 Starts)
First choice and consistent for so long. Had a small
dip in form mid-season but recovered and even
scored one of his trademark goals in his final game.

Kalvin Phillips   29 Appearances (28 Starts)
Mr. Consistency, who is well worth his England
caps. He gives everything and consequently picks
up the odd injury.

Raphinha   30 Appearances (26 Starts)
Must be the bargain of the season and another great
find by Victor Orta. Should be a real star in the
Premier League next time out.

Liam Cooper   **25 Appearances (25 Starts)**
A dependable and solid captain. One of the top
beneficiaries of Marcelo Bielsa's coaching.

Pascal Struijk   **27 Appearances (22 Starts)**
Another major success story. Breakthrough season
for another youngster with the world at his feet.

Tyler Roberts   **27 Appearances (14 Starts)**
Had a slow start and took a while to re-establish
himself, but when he did he was worth his place.
Needs to score more goals and be given better luck.

Rodrigo   **26 Appearances (14 Starts)**
A season disrupted by illness and injury. He came
good towards the end with four goals in three games
and is beginning to show what a class act he is.

Diego Llorente   **15 Appearances (14 Starts)**
Originally bedevilled by injuries, but has proved to
be one of the league's most polished centre backs. A
great positional player with impeccable distribution.

Helder Costa   **22 Appearances (13 Starts)**
Although overshadowed a little following the
arrival of Raphinha, he continues to deliver the
goods when called upon.

Robin Koch   **17 Appearances (13 Starts)**
Grew in stature after a shaky start. Eventually had
to succumb to the injury he was carrying. Returned
even stronger and may be versatile enough to
deputise for Kalvin Phillips when required.

Pablo Hernandez   16 Appearances (3 Starts)

Probably not the season that Pablo would have chosen as his final one with Club. Blighted by injury and rarely able to give of his best.

Jamie Shackleton   13 Appearances (3 Starts)

He will be disappointed with his lack of progress. Frustrated by injuries, this youngster still has a lot to give. Next season will be an important for him.

Kiko Casilla   3 Appearances (3 Starts)

The controversial keeper has generally done what was asked of him when selected, but his future remains uncertain.

Gaetano Berardi   2 Appearances (1 Start)

A hard working defender, who's season has also been blighted with injuries. One of the favourites who will be missed by the Elland Road faithful.

Ian Poveda   14 Appearances (0 Starts)

Seems on the edge of a breakthrough, but still has a lot to learn. He couldn't be in a better place!

Leif Davis   2 Appearances (0 Starts)

Left back that can also play as another central defender. He had a great season in the Under 23s.

Niall Huggins   1 Appearance (0 Starts)

Another defender who's a regular in the Under 23s and got some minutes in the away match at Arsenal.

Every team that is promoted to the Premier League has one major objective and that is to stay there. Leeds United are no exception to this.

The fallout rate is alarming and doesn't improve as the years go by. Of the three teams that were relegated in 2020-21, only Fulham had much of a chance of staying alive once Easter had arrived.

Although aware of the increase in media hype that comes with life in the Premier League, most of us did not truly understand what it was really like until we experienced it. Marcelo Bielsa himself had deep concerns about what was required of him in terms of media commitments.

Indeed, it was one of the most contentious issues on the new contract which he signed on the eve of this season. For United, it started off with praise for their swashbuckling style after their remarkable performance in the first game against Liverpool.

The fact that this praise was a little bit patronising was probably only to be expected for a newly promoted side.

As the season progressed, the praise began to be mixed with a few sneers about United's inability to defend well in this division. Not one pundit alluded to the fact that the Whites had a makeshift defence for much of the first half of the season.

The ladies and gentlemen of the media merely pointed to the plethora of statistics that United were poor at defending set pieces and were shipping goals like they were going out of fashion.

Even when United had a settled defence and the 'goals against' tally started to go down impressively, the media put this down to their perception that Bielsa had been compelled to change his tactics. Presumably, they thought that it was because he had listened to their advice!

Of course, facts are facts but nobody sought to pinpoint the reasons why these things were happening. One 'smart alec' even accused one of the best coaches in the world of employing naïve tactics. Most of these so-called journalists behave with all the intelligence and tact of spotty, shiny suited teenage mobile phone sales people.

Most Premier League coaches would have put their interviewers straight in no uncertain terms and would have given the reasons. Some even spend more time whining and whinging that their interrogators end up avoiding these types of comments. Marcelo Bielsa never offers excuses however valid the excuses may be.

He never criticises match officials, players from other teams and when his own team has lost, if he feels that the loss is deserved, he blames himself. To operate in the way he does takes almost superhuman self-control and discipline.

He doesn't reply directly in English because he knows that his replies will be manipulated, but despite this his answers to questions are well thought out and are far wiser than those of his contemporaries.

The other things that tried Bielsa's patience were the frequently repeated myths.

"Bielsa's sides 'burn out' and run out of steam towards the end of a season."

"Bielsa doesn't care about the result as long as they play attractive football."

"Bielsa's players are prone to developing more injuries than other teams owing to the intensity of the way they play and train."

"Bielsa's insistence on a small squad leaves a team vulnerable."

These are just a few examples of the stuff endlessly repeated by people who should know better. Proper research is so easy nowadays and yet most would prefer to just repeat things that they have heard elsewhere. In some ways, this nonsense has helped United. I really believe that the wins in the second half of the season, particularly against Manchester City and Spurs were assisted by the fact that some of their expensive players really believed that United were naïve defensively.

175

The penny will probably drop next season but at least the media can console themselves with 'second season syndrome' and comparisons with Sheffield United.

Marcelo Bielsa is a builder of teams. He is a developer of players. United fans do not sit about nervously waiting to see if he will massage his ego by accepting a big money offer from one of their rivals, nationally or internationally.

He is demanding, aggressive and tenacious. Players respect him for what he has helped them to achieve. United's wonderful season has come about by the hard work of the players and the sheer genius of Marcelo Bielsa.

Next year, the challenges will be tougher but there is a core group of players who have been together for three seasons. This group has and will be augmented with carefully chosen players who have the ability and also the foresight to buy into the project.

Marcelo Bielsa has been with United longer than with any other club side. There is a powerful synergy between him and the other 'Fantastic Four' members, Andrea Radrizzani, Angus Kinnear and Victor Orta. Long may it continue.

Once again Marcelo, muchas gracias for all you have done for Leeds United and the supporters.

I am once again indebted to my grandson, George Gill, for his editing skills and unwavering ability to keep me on track!

Printed in Great Britain
by Amazon